W9-ARU-164

The ISLLC Standards in Action

A Principal's Handbook

Carol M. Engler, Ph.D.

EYE ON EDUCATION
6 DEPOT WAY WEST, SUITE 106
LARCHMONT, NY 10538
(914) 833–0551
(914) 833–0761 fax
www.eyeoneducation.com

Library of Congress Cataloging-in-Publication Data

Engler, Carol M., 1948-
    The ISLLC standards in action : principal's handbook / Carol M. Engler.
        p. cm.
    Includes bibliographical references.
    ISBN 1-930556-77-2
    1. School management and organization--United States. 2. School administrators--United States. 3. Educational leadership--Standards--United States. I. Interstate School Leaders Licensure Consortium. II. Title.

LB2805.E534 2004
371.2--dc22   2004043217

10 9 8 7 6 5 4 3 2 1

Editorial and production services provided by
Richard H. Adin Freelance Editorial Services
52 Oakwood Blvd., Poughkeepsie, NY 12603-4112
(914-471-3566)

This book is dedicated to
S.E.R
In laughter and love

Acknowledgments

This handbook is the result of tremendous efforts by individuals who believe that the future of our nation belongs to the next generation of educational leaders. I would like to offer a special word of thanks to the following leaders:

Carla Edlefson, Ph.D., Professor of Educational Administration, Ashland University, Ashland, Ohio

Fred Fastenau, Associate Executive Director, Ohio Association of Secondary School Administrators

Janet Kearney, Ph.D., Assistant Professor, Educational Administration, Ashland University, Ashland, Ohio

Paul Kulik, Ph.D., Deputy Superintendent, Franklin County Educational Service Center, Columbus, Ohio

Kay Meyer, Ph.D., Professor, Department of Sociology and Faculty Associate, John Glenn Institute for Public Policy and Public Service, The Ohio State University, Columbus, Ohio

Steven E. Raines, Executive Director, The Ohio Association of Secondary School Administrators

Sherry Lahr, Ph.D., Associate/Adjunct Professor, Educational Leadership, Ashland University, Ashland, Ohio

Tom Romack, Assistant Superintendent, Mahoning County Educational Service Center, Youngstown, Ohio

Sylvester Small, Ed.D., Superintendent, Akron Public Schools, Akron, Ohio

Sara Stanley, Ph.D., Former Principal, Central-Hower High School, Akron Public Schools, Akron, Ohio

Table of Contents

Introduction

Job Title: Principal Teacher
Job Description: Oversee attendance and enrollment
figures and the general cleanliness of the school.
                    (Hessel, & Holloway, 2002, p. 11)

In 1839, a banner year for schools, the nation's first school principal was hired in Cincinnati, Ohio. The job description sent a clear message that the school's leader need not have any delusions of visionary leadership.

The evolution of the responsibilities of America's public school principals has gone from custodial responsibilities, to day-to-day crisis management, to its present position of instructional leadership. This new mantle of educational leadership, however, is still in its infancy.

With the advent of the school reform movement that began with the release of *A Nation At Risk* in 1983, standards-based curriculum became a prime consideration in all curriculum areas. However, the nation's principals were literally left out of the loop in the early days of the school reform movement when emphasis was placed primarily on curriculum standards as reflected in the classroom teacher's delivery of instruction. It was not until 1994 that standards for principals were formally introduced into the reform movement.

In 1994, the Council of Chief State School Officers (CCSSO) created the Interstate School Leaders Licensure Consortium (ISLLC), whose charge was to address the issue of standards in the field of educational leadership (Hackmann, 2002). The ISLLC standards, a set of six research-based standards, were consciously developed to focus "on matters of learning and teaching and the creation of powerful learning environments". (ISLLC, 1996, p.8). These standards were deliberately broad, placing emphasis on the knowledge, dispositions, and performances necessary for exemplary school leadership.

The ISLLC standards are a commendable achievement by its architects. They reflect a depth and breadth of content that encompasses the wide spectrum of knowledge that the contemporary principal can use as a benchmark for professional excellence.

These six ISLLC standards emphasize the belief that school administrators must ensure the success of all students by:

1. Facilitating the development, articulation, implementation, and stewardship of a vision of learning that is shared and supported by the school community

2. Advocating, nurturing, and sustaining a school culture and instructional program conducive to student learning and staff professional growth

3. Ensuring management of the organization, operations, and resources for a safe, efficient, and effective learning environment

4. Collaborating with families and community members, responding to diverse community interests and needs, and mobilizing community resources

5. Acting with integrity, fairness, and in an ethical manner

6. Understanding, responding to, and influencing the larger political, social, economic, legal, and cultural context (ISLLC, 1996)

Although it was the desire of the consortium to raise the bar for the practice of school leadership, the ISLLC standards were also developed to be compatible with the new National Council for the Accreditation of Teacher Education (NCATE) Curriculum Guidelines. In this way, educational leaders once and for all left the domain of "management" and entered the unchartered territory of "leadership."

Purpose of this Book

With the development and acceptance of the ISLLC Standards as licensure and professional development guidelines in 44 states, beginning and veteran principals, along with graduate students in educational administration, have faced the excitement and challenge of reframing their own beliefs on the nature and practice of leadership. Although much has been written about the knowledge and application of the ISLLC standards, the topic of *actual job performance* is relatively new.

Busy educational leaders need "hands on" professional development that is not only designed to increase student achievement and improve school climate and culture, but also to serve as a means for enhancing their own leadership capabilities.

The purpose of this handbook is threefold:

1. To help beginning and experienced principals understand and advance their own professional development and licensure plans using practical activities that can be accomplished within the framework of the busy school year

2. To educate current educational administration graduate students on the ISLLC standards and how those standards can be implemented into their future roles as leaders

3. To instruct university faculty in principal preparation programs on how the ISLLC standards can be applied to problem-based learning courses

The Real World of the ISLLC Standards

Over 160 individuals contributed to this book. Graduate students in Educational Administration at the Columbus Center of Ashland University participated in designing and writing this book as a class assignment in the course, *Introduction to Educational Administration*. The graduate students were asked to interview school administrators, research Web sites, read books, and brainstorm with their colleagues for real-world ideas and suggestions for implementing each ISLLC standard. Their re-search, far-reaching and inspiring, resulted in this book of strat-egies. Each of Chapters 1 through 6 addresses an ISLLC stan-dard. The chapter titles are my attempt to help administrators learn the main idea of each standard in an easy-to-remember format. In addition, each strategy carries with it links to other ISLLC standards.

What began as this instructor's desire for students to under-stand and be able to implement the ISLLC standards through practical strategies has become a handbook for busy principals, professors, and graduate students everywhere.

Please use this handbook as it was intended. It is written in a user-friendly format so that busy educators can refer to it and access usable ideas within a few minutes. This book is not meant to gather dust. It has been written to enhance the performance of all educational leaders.

Carol M. Engler, Ph.D.
Assistant Professor
Educational Administration
Ashland University
Ashland, Ohio

Contributors

Assistant Professor: Dr. Janet Kearney

Adjunct Professors: Dr. Paul Kulik, Fred Fastenau

Graduate Student Editor: Jennifer Moorefield

Chapter 1: Vision Values

Graduate Students: Jay Baker, Cheryl Barker, Mike Barron, Linda Bennett, Jaime Blair, Max Eisl, Bob Gibson, Kyle Gibson, Dora Higgenbotham, Patricia Jenkins, Adam Kunkle, Jennifer Moorefield, Kerrie Schweinfurth, Janet Smith, Joshua Straus, Lisa Patton, Kyle Walters

Administrators: Phillip Binkley, Gail Buick, Dr. Steve Castle, Debra Clauss, Linda Gregg, Dr. J. L. High, Katie Huenke, Bob Jackson, Carol King, Maryann Sweeney, Lee Ann Yoakum

Chapter 2: Culture Counts

Graduate Students: Brenda Custodio, Lisa Frasure, Robb Gonda, Amber Hejtmancik, Jeff Hempleman, Judy McCombs, Dawn Mather, Christine Michael, Lynda Nabors, Travis Rupp, Jonathan Stevens, Candyce Switzer, Carol Trimble, David Ware, Diana Whitehead

Administrators: Dwight Carter, Debra Clauss, John Crerand, Brice Frasure, James Grube, Keith Richards, Madeline Partlow, Pam VanHorn

Chapter 3: Safe and Sound

Graduate Students: Adam Beggrow, Curt Brogan, Kathy Colasanti, Tracey Colson, Andy Cox, Matt Cox, Kevin Cutler, Matthew Dill, Henry Hale, David Harmon, Joseph Jude, Ruth Kotler, Danielle Lee, Brian Luthy, Michelle Manley, Tonya Milligan, Mike Palmer, Jamie Scott

Administrators: Mike Beck, Christine Cline, John Lanka, Chris Lester, David Kenley, Richard Littell, Carl Martin, Steve Mazzi

Chapter 4: Community Connections

Graduate Students: Paul Bailey, Sara Busch, Leslie Charlemagne, Carol Comanita, Pam Eberhardt, Dr. Jan Federenko, Paul Galloway, Lori Giuliani, Bryant Hall, Ron Hairston, Lane Halterman, Ron Hairston, Anna Telerski-McClung, George Mosholder, Stephanie Porta, Allyson Price, Jennifer Schneider, Ronda Stewart, Cindy Teske, Cyndi Toledo

Administrators: Bob Britton, Roger Collins, Bev Downing, Suellen Fitzwater, Ron Hairston, Mike McCreary, Dr. Gail Mitchell, Krista Morelli, Richard Vance

Chapter 5: Ethics Embodied

Graduate Students: Aaron Butler, Billie Sue Dunn, Kellie Edwards, Marc Erhart, Jason Griffith, LeAnthony Jones, Julie Kenney, Beth Lutz, Sheila Martin, Nancy McClelland, Stan McDonald, Tom McDonnell, Brian Meyer, Jennifer Ross, Wes Weaver, Jay Wolfe, Michele Wyatt

Administrators: Barbara Blake, Stan Embry, Mindy Farry, Deborah Kozlesky, Dr. Sherry Lahr, Jim Liddle, Debra Odom, Steve Raines, Dr. Sylvester Small, William Whitlatch
Attorney: Richard Mann

Chapter 6: Politics, Please

Graduate Students: Jennifer Decker, Tom Fry, Amy Gooding, Robert Griffith, Jeff Lavin, Brian Lidle, Angela Martin, Jim Miller, Sherri Mitko, Vicki Moss, Mark Mousa, Christopher Pae, Theresa Pettis, Michael Roberts, Christina Schwartz, Jaime Taylor, Barbara Travis, David Whitt, Matthew Wilson

Administrators: Jeff Brown, Gail Buick, James Grube, Stan Embry, Julie Kenney, Carol King, Peggy McMurry, Steve Mazzi, Andrew Smith, Jane Vazquez, Kristin Whiting, Kyle Wolfe

Guidance Counselor: Tom Woodford

1
Vision Values:
ISLLC Standard 1

"A school administrator is an educational leader who promotes the success of all students by facilitating the development, articulation, implementation, and stewardship of a vision of learning that is shared and supported by the school community."

Develop a Vision Statement

Goals

- Have a road map on which the entire school community can focus its time and energy.
- Engage the school community in building the school from the ground up.
- Empower all stakeholders to participate in shared decision making.

Links with Other ISLLC Standards

#2 Culture Counts

#4 Community Connections

#5 Ethics Embodied

Resource

Debra Clauss, Principal
Mount Gilead High School
338 Park Avenue
Mount Gilead, OH 43338
E-mail: deb_c@treca.org

Keep in Mind

- Include all major school community stakeholders.
- Set a time frame for completion of the statement. It is easy to keep adding "one more thing" to the statement until the vision becomes muddled.
- Ensure that the vision statement is a vivid description of the organization. It needs to be something that people can visualize down the road.
- Create a vision statement that the entire school community can state and talk about. Keep it short, sweet, and realistic so that gains toward achieving the vision can be measured in small successes.

Communicate the Vision

Goals

- Spread the word to the entire community about the school's vision.
- Instill a sense of pride in teachers and students that the vision is worthy of public attention.
- Ensure that no matter who the principal is in later years, the vision becomes a fixture in the school culture.

Links with Other ISLLC Standards

#2 Culture Counts

#4 Community Connections

#6 Politics, Please

Resource

The Wellington School
3650 Reed Road
Columbus, OH 43220
Web site: www.wellington.org

Keep in Mind

- Since the vision statement sets a clear path for the strategic plan of the school, decide on the most effective way of communicating it to community members within your school district. Some of the communication options to consider are community meetings, newspaper, radio, television coverage, and an Internet Web site.
- Have a long-range plan for communication of the vision statement. To be truly effective, the statement needs to be repeated over a period of time.

Host a Community Night

Goals

- Build into the school calendar an annual event that will communicate the vision of the school.
- Give students the belief that they are at the very heart of the school's vision.
- Enable staff to work as a team in communicating "kids come first."

Links with Other ISLLC Standards

#2 Culture Counts

#4 Community Connections

#6 Politics, Please

Resource

Bob Jackson, Principal
Franklin Heights High School
1001 Demorest Road
Columbus, OH 43204
Web site: www.swcs.k12.oh.us/fhhs.htm

Keep in Mind

- This event is designed to allow all students to shine by allowing students to conduct the entire evening.
- Student teams put together presentations about what they have learned throughout the school year. The presentations may include posters, PowerPoint presentations, booklets, and so on.
- Invitees include parents, staff members, students, families, central office employees, media reporters, board members, and community leaders.
- The planning committee can consist of adult/student representatives from grade levels or teams within the building.

Build Strong Business Partnerships

Goals

- Engage business power brokers in the education of the community's most vital resource: its children.
- Establish a communication network to assist in keeping up to date on the community's perception of the school.
- Provide networking opportunities for adults and children that goes beyond the boundaries of the school walls.

Links with Other ISLLC Standards:

#2 Culture Counts

#4 Community Connections

#6 Politics, Please

Resources

Loudoun County Public Schools
102 North Street, NW
Leesburg, VA 20176
School-Business Partnerships
Web site: www.loudoun.k12.va.us

Keep in Mind

- Business partnerships communicate a powerful message to students that school is vital to success in life.
- Businesses offer schools resources to assist in teaching complex concepts, expertise in carrying out projects, guest speakers who can serve as positive role models, and connections to the world of work.
- Some of the best programs, such as Tech Prep and Junior Achievement, provide applications-based, hands-on training that emphasizes teamwork and critical thinking.

Utilize Vertical Teams

Goals

- Encourage effective communication between all professionals in the school district.
- Emphasize that the vision of a district extends beyond the borders of each individual school.
- Celebrate small successes in pursuit of the school's vision.

Links with Other ISLLC Standards

#2 Culture Counts

#4 Community Connections

#6 Politics, Please

Resource

Carol King, Principal
John Sells Middle School
150 W. Bridge St.
Dublin, OH 43016
Web site: www.dublinschools.net

Keep in Mind

- Vertical teams are an excellent method to help teachers grow and network professionally.
- Development opportunities include a late-start day four times a year dedicated to "vertical teams" in which teachers across the district meet with other teachers from similar curricular areas to map out interdisciplinary units.
- Guest speakers attend biweekly meetings at individual schools, presenting information that can unite teachers in reaching the school's vision.

Create an Academic Awards Night

Goals

- Reward the success of students by making their progress a cause for celebration.
- Communicate to the larger community the purpose of the school's vision.
- Send the message to all students that academics deserve public recognition.

Links with Other ISLLC Standards:

#2 Culture Counts

#4 Community Connections

#6 Politics, Please

Resource

Gilbert Public Schools
140 S. Gilbert Road
Gilbert, AZ 85296
Web site: www.gilbert.k12.az.us

Keep in Mind

- This event is a district-wide program that acknowledges and honors students in grades 4-6 who have achieved and maintained high academic standing during the current school year.
- A student must have received no more than one "B." All other grades must be "A's." Subject areas are reading, written language, math, science/health, and social studies.
- Students must have earned an evaluation of at least a "good" grade in self-management.

Salute Student Contributions in Many Areas

Goals

- Encourage all kinds of student contributions to the school community.
- Engage the community in recognition of all students' unique talents.
- Showcase the vision of the school as a place where each student deserves recognition for a job well done.

Links with Other ISLLC Standards:

#2 Culture Counts

#4 Community Connections

#6 Politics, Please

Resource

Marysville Middle School
833 N. Maple Street
Marysville, OH 43040
Web site: www.marysville.k12.oh.us/mms

Keep in Mind

- This award is not limited to academic achievement. Every month, each staff member has the opportunity to nominate a student for the Mighty Monarch award. Students can be nominated for consistently good work or behavior, for an improvement in work or behavior, for an exceptionally good job on a test or project, or for helping others.
- Recipients are given recognition with an ice cream party organized by parents, a folder filled with prizes, acknowledgment in the local newspaper, their names on the school Web site and their pictures displayed on a bulletin board outside the school office area.

Learn to Write Grants

Goals

- Supplement school monies for projects focusing on student achievement.
- Spread the word to the larger community that the vision of the school is viable enough to undergo public scrutiny.
- Provide teacher leaders with the tools to enhance their students' learning.

Links with Other ISLLC Standards

#2 Culture Counts
#4 Community Connections
#6 Politics, Please

Resource

Nystrom
A Division of Herff Jones, Inc.
3333 Elston Avenue
Chicago, IL 60618
Web site: www.nystromnet.com

Keep in Mind

- Implementation of the vision and mission of the school can be costly without outside resources. Grant monies are available through numerous sources.
- After a grant is awarded, the stipulations and administration of the grant are crucial to its success. Be sure to check the grant rules carefully regarding limitations on how monies are to be spent.

Map Your Community's Resources

Goals

- Educate all stakeholders in the wealth of community resources available to schools.
- Serve as a time-saving method when particular services need to be contacted.
- Engage the wider community in the vision of the school.

Links with Other ISLLC Standards

#2 Culture Counts

#4 Community Connections

#6 Politics, Please

Resource

Katie Huenke, Coordinator, Office of Student Assistance Intervention and Outreach
Columbus City Schools
270 E. State St., Columbus, OH 43215
E-mail: khuenke@columbus.k12.oh.us
Web site: UCLA/School Mental Health Project: www.smhp.psych. ucla.edu

Keep in Mind

- Just as curriculum mapping is essential in helping schools increase student achievement, resource mapping can help identify and coordinate school and community resources.
- Many times, community resources are overlapping, overlooked, or underused.
- Entire districts may want to investigate this method of community resource mapping as district needs evolve over time.

Sponsor an Awards Breakfast

Goals

- Give special recognition to students who have been caught doing something great.
- Send the message to students that good behavior deserves recognition.
- Involve the business community in the school's vision.

Links with Other ISLLC Standards

#2 Culture Counts

#4 Community Connections

#6 Politics, Please

Resource

Linda Gregg, Principal
Arrowhead Elementary School
2385 Hollenback Rd.
Lewis Center, OH 43035
E-mail: MDLRGregg@cs.com

Keep in Mind

- This is not necessarily an academic award for students. It can help to recognize students who might otherwise "slip through the cracks" in terms of recognition.
- All adults in the school can nominate students for this recognition. This will engage and involve the noninstructional staff as well as teachers.
- Community businesses can donate prizes for this event.

Give First Graders a Reason to Celebrate Literacy

Goals

- Give first graders a head start on participating in special recognition activities.
- Encourage parents to read with their children.
- Engage parents in a positive relationship with the school.

Links with Other ISLLC Standards

#2 Culture Counts

#4 Community Connections

#6 Politics, Please

Resource

Marion City Schools
910 E. Church St.
Marion, OH 43302-4396
Web site: www.marioncity.k12.oh.us

Keep in Mind

- This evening is a special time that first graders and their parents can share together.
- This event gives parents the chance to partner with the school in literacy efforts without labeling students who need special help.
- A story that can be of interest to all is read aloud by a teacher and comprehension activities follow.
- Parents have the opportunity to learn a variety of reading activities that they can use at home with their children.
- Each child receives a book to take home.

Create Student-Led Parent Conferences

Goals

- Put students in charge of communication with parents and teachers regarding student progress.
- Give students the chance to highlight their organizational and communication skills.
- Give parents and students the responsibility and the power to communicate about academic issues.

Links with Other ISLLC Standards

#2 Culture Counts

#4 Community Connection

#5 Ethics Embodied

Resource

Maryann Sweeney, Principal
Marysville Middle School
833 N Maple St.
Marysville, OH 43040
E-mail: msweeney@marysville.k12.oh.us

Keep in Mind

- This student-led effort takes the place of the traditional parent-teacher conference.
- Students create portfolios to reflect their progress. The portfolios may contain any of the following: work samples, reflections, and self-evaluation/teacher evaluations.
- This is a great opportunity for students to engage in open and honest dialogue with their parents and teachers.

Begin a BUGS and BATS Program

Goals

- Encourage improvement in grades and attitude for students with a unique and catchy phrase.
- Refuse to label students by grades alone.
- Help students strive to improve throughout the entire school year.

Links with Other ISLLC Standards

#2 Culture Counts

#4 Community Connections

Resource

Gail Buick, Principal
Salem Elementary School
1040 Garvey Rd.
Columbus, OH 43229
Phone: (614) 365-5351

Keep in Mind

- The BUGS Award (Bringing Up Grades Successfully) is given to students who show improvement each grading period.
- Students must improve at least one letter grade.
- The BATS Award (Better Attitude Toward School) is given to students who have shown an improved attitude toward school during the previous grading period. This improvement can be demonstrated by a decrease in absences, tardiness, or disciplinary referrals.

Invite the Community to Dinner

Goals

- Create dialogue and collegiality between the school and larger community.
- Bring stakeholders to the school in an effort to showcase student work.
- Begin a long-range planning process in a collegial atmosphere.

Links with Other ISLLC Standards

#2 Culture Counts

#4 Community Connections

#6 Politics, Please

Resource

Knowledge Works Foundation
One West Fourth St.
Suite 200
Cincinnati, OH 45202
Web site: www.kwfdn.org

Keep in Mind

- These dinners are an opportunity for community members to voice their opinions.
- A third-party facilitator serves as emcee for the evening.
- After dinner is served, the facilitator leads an open discussion on topics about which the school would like the community's input.
- A second facilitator may collect ideas on an easel or in PowerPoint.
- Ideas are then categorized and presented to the school as a whole for analysis.

Design a Mission Statement Rubric

Goals

- Measure and evaluate the current state of the school's mission.
- Keep staff and community informed of the school's mission through use of the rubric.
- Establish a school culture that welcomes inquiry into school practices.
- Take the school's mission statement into the public arena for dialogue and discussion.

Links with Other ISLLC Standards

#2 Culture Counts
#4 Community Connections
#6 Politics, Please

Resource

Technology Assistance for Kansas Educators
Kansas State Department of Education
120 SE 10th Avenue, Topeka, KS 66612-1182
Web site: www.taken.org/techplanrubric

Keep in Mind

- Develop a rubric and then rate your school as "Excellent," "Effective," or "[needing] Continuous Improvement" in achieving your school's vision.
- Use the rubric at the beginning of each school year.
- Include answers to the following questions in the rubric:
  - Is there schoolwide knowledge of the vision?
  - Have goals been developed to achieve the vision?
  - Have objectives been developed to meet the goals?
  - Is there a proposal to integrate the vision more completely into the learning environment?

Display a Mission Statement Banner

Goals

- Publicize the mission statement of the school to everyone who enters.
- Set a tone of high expectations to the entire community.
- Provide a daily reminder to all students and staff of the school's mission.

Links with Other ISLLC Standards

#2 Culture Counts

#3 Safe and Sound

#4 Community Connections

#6 Politics, Please

Reference

Dr. J. L. High, Associate Professor of Education
Lipscomb University
3901 Granny White Pike
Nashville, TN 37204-3951
E-mail: highjl@lipscomb.edu

Keep in Mind

- Have a commercial printer create a large banner with the school's mission statement.
- Display the banner over the front door of the building for each student and all visitors to see as they arrive at school.

Develop a District-Wide Technology Plan

Goals

- Integrate technology into the vision of each school.
- Make technology compatible with state curriculum guidelines.
- Establish partnerships with community resources that can serve as technology advisors.

Links with Other ISLLC Standards

#2 Culture Counts

#4 Community Connections

#6 Politics, Please

Resource

Dr. Steve Castle, Superintendent
Delaware City Schools
248 N Washington St.
Delaware, OH 43015
E-mail: castle@dcs.k12.oh.us

Keep in Mind

- Set a tone for students and staff that will encourage them to use electronic tools on a regular basis.
- Provide training and support so all will take advantage of technology.
- Create an expectation that students will use software and hardware to gather and report information in all curriculum areas for research and decision making.
- Design mentoring and support groups to assist staff in integrating technology into all phases of their work.

Salute Staff Efforts

Goals

- Call public attention to staff members who strive to achieve the school vision.
- Send a message to the entire community that the school vision is attainable.
- Set the tone for learning with students who see their teachers as role models for the school vision implementation.

Other ISLLC Standards

#2 Culture Counts

#3 Safe and Sound

#4 Community Connections

#6 Politics, Please

Resource

Phillip Binkley, Government Affairs Assistant
% The Ohio Association of Secondary School
    Administrators
8050 N High Street, Suite 180
Columbus, OH 43235-6484
E-mail: p_binkley@sbcglobal.net

Keep in Mind

- Develop an "Apple for the Teacher" Award.
- Notify members of the school community that they may suggest staff members for the award.
- Include reasons the teacher should be recognized in all nominations.
- Create a paper apple on which the principal writes the teacher's accomplishments along with the nominator's name.
- Place the paper apple in a designated area such as a trophy case or bulletin board.

Hold a Dress Code Fashion Show

Goals

- Help students visualize what the dress code looks like.
- Create a light-hearted activity to present the serious topic of the school dress code.
- Enable students, parents, and staff to communicate with one another about the purpose of the dress code.

Links to Other ISLLC Standards

#2 Culture Counts

#3 Safe and Sound

#4 Community Connections

#6 Politics, Please

Resource

Lee Ann Yoakum, Principal
Groveport Madison Middle School North
5474 Sedalia Dr.
Groveport, OH 43232
E-mail: leayoakum@hotmail.com

Keep in Mind

- At the beginning of each school year, a Back-to-School Evening is held.
- Students model the latest violations of the dress code.
- An announcer provides commentary.
- Parents and students experience a humorous evening and at the same time learn of the dress code and the consequences for dress-code violations.

Have an Inclusion Cookout

Goals

- Provide an informal format for the inclusion program's staff, students, and parents to get to know one another.
- Make sure that everyone is on the same page with the school regarding the format of the inclusion program.
- Help students adjust to inclusion program activities before the first day of school.

Links with Other ISLLC Standards

#2 Culture Counts

#3 Safe and Sound

#4 Community Connections

#6 Politics, Please

Resource

National Education Association
1201 16th Street NW
Washington, D.C. 20036-3290
Web site: www.nea.org

Keep in Mind

- The picnic is available to anyone in the school community who has ties to the inclusion program.
- The event might be held in mid-August at a local park away from the school building.
- After the cookout, teachers that are a part of the inclusion team will talk to the parents and students about what school will be like in the fall. PowerPoint and handouts can be used.
- After the presentation, participants should engage in an open discussion on inclusion topics.

2
Culture Counts: ISLLC Standard 2

"A school administrator is an educational leader who promotes the success of all students by advocating, nurturing, and sustaining a school culture and instructional program conducive to student learning and staff professional growth."

Learn about the Culture

Goals

- Determine what the expectations are for student achievement.
- Find out what the staff expects of themselves as professionals.
- Discover what kind of pace is necessary in implementing change.
- Learn what the staff and students would like to see in the way of change.

Links to Other ISLLC Standards

#1 Vision Values 　　　#4 Community Connections
#3 Safe and Sound 　　#6 Politics, Please

Resource

Bulach, C. R. (2001, April). A 4-step process for identifying and reshaping school culture. (Publisher: The National Association of Secondary School Principals), *Principal Leadership I(8)*.

Keep in Mind

- An informal expectations diagnosis is less threatening for staff members when the principal is new to the building.
- The secret for successful change is identifying an existing culture and reshaping it.
- Including all members of the school community (such as students, faculty, and uncertified staff) in the diagnosis will provide the principal with balanced viewpoints.
- Be sure that the school culture is diagnosed on a regular and ongoing basis in order to receive the most enlightening feedback.

Diversify Culturally Within the Academic Program

Goals

- Teach an awareness of different cultures to the school community.
- Develop an attitude of tolerance for all cultures.
- Find a way to reduce conflict through an appreciation of different cultures.

Links with Other ISLLC Standards

#1 Vision Values

#3 Safe and Sound

#4 Community Connections

Resource

Brimijoin, K., Marquissee, E., & Tomlinson, C. A. (2003, February). Using data to differentiate instruction. (Published by: Association for Supervision and Curriculum Development). *Educational Leadership, 60*(5).

Keep in Mind

- Incorporating multicultural arts, music, and drama in fine arts courses sets the stage for understanding cultural diversity.
- Promoting diversity through aggressive hiring of a multiethnic staff sends a strong signal that cultural diversity is honored.
- Creating opportunities for students to experience diversity through cultural exchange programs, both locally and globally, sets a tone that diversity is not just something that is read about in textbooks.

Promote Alternative Assessment Strategies

Goals

- Set the tone for acceptance and celebration of multiple forms of intelligence.
- Encourage research-based classroom instruction that encourages critical thinking skills in students.
- Ask professional staff to serve as role models to students in outside-the-box thinking.

Links with Other ISLLC Strategies

#1 Vision Values

#4 Community Connections

#5 Ethics Embodied

#6 Politics, Please

Resource

Guskey, T. (2003, February). How classroom assessments improve learning. (Published by: Association for Supervision and Curriculum Development). *Educational Leadership, 60*(5).

Keep in Mind

- Allow teachers time in staff meetings to share assessment techniques.
- Encourage portfolio assessment in appropriate classes.
- Promote multiple forms of assessment that complement district and state data.
- Encourage informal assessment in daily instruction.
- Use alternative forms of assessment to evaluate schoolwide progress toward goals.

Initiate Adult Learning
and Professional Development Models

Goals

- Provide opportunities for staff to delve into their own learning styles.
- Serve as a role model for staff by using your own learning style's strengths and challenges as an example of leadership style.
- Promote teambuilding with the professional staff.

Links with Other ISLLC Standards

#1 Vision Values

#4 Community Connections

#5 Ethics Embodied

Resource

Keirsey, D.(1998). *Please Understand Me II*. Del Mar, CA: Prometheus Nemesis Press.

Keep in Mind

- A retreat setting provides a relaxing atmosphere for working with staff.
- The staff needs to understand that adult learning styles are just as important as children's learning styles.
- When staff feels free to explore their own learning styles, team-building activities can then become part of professional development.
- Conflict can be minimized by using the safe framework of this Myers-Briggs type format.
- Teachers can develop their own lesson plans around the unique learning styles of their students.

Hold Faculty and Staff Book Talks

Goals

- Emphasize lifelong learning with staff.
- Provide adult time for staff to share their ideas.
- Send a message to students that teachers are also learners.
- Transmit to the larger community that the school is a community of learners.

Links with Other ISLLC Standards

#1 Vision Values

#4 Community Connections

#5 Ethics Embodied

#6 Politics, Please

Resource

Grandview Heights City Schools
1587 West Third Avenue, Columbus, OH 43212-2873
Web site: www.grandviewschools.org

Keep in Mind

- The principal or superintendent can assign one book for the staff to read and discuss during the school year.
- The book is provided by the district or school to each employee.
- Monies for the books can be obtained through business partners if there are no professional development monies available.
- The book can be discussed throughout the school year at staff and school district meetings.
- The selection of the book should address a need such as morale, organization, time management, professional empowerment, or preparation for change within the work environment.

Be an Invitational Principal

Goals

- Encourage teacher empowerment.
- Set a tone of generosity and respect with the staff.
- Role model the idea of shared power with teachers.
- Publicize the accomplishments of the staff to the larger community.

Links with Other ISLLC Standards

#1 Vision Values

#4 Community Connections

#5 Ethics Embodied

Resource

Hopkins, G. 25 ways to motivate teachers. *The Principal Files,* from www.educationworld.com

Keep in Mind

- Let all staff members have a turn at your parking spot.
- Recognize staff members/students/parents who go above and beyond the call of duty by using memos, notes, and small gifts to express your appreciation.
- Incorporate a luncheon/early dinner/breakfast into a staff meeting. Play relaxing music during this time.
- Have teachers select a colleague for the Golden Apple award at a staff meeting each month, to be given to an individual who has done an especially fine job the previous month.
- Hold an Educational Olympics once a year where teachers compete in athletic and nonathletic teambuilding activities, such as helping one another through a maze or participating in a relay team.

Keep It Light

Goals

- Make school fun for adults as well a children.
- Create a positive and relaxed atmosphere among staff.
- Begin a staff tradition that becomes part of the school's history.
- Set a congenial tone for future collaborative efforts on behalf of students.

Links with Other ISLLC Standards

#1 Vision Values

Resource

John Crerand, Principal
Alexander Graham Bell School
1455 Huy Rd.
Columbus, OH 43224
Phone: (614) 365-5977

Keep in Mind

- At Christmas, hold a staff party off school property. It can be a luncheon or dinner event. Make sure it is very informal so that people will have a chance to see one another in a stress-free environment.
- Each person brings a gift...maybe some item that they want to get rid of. The only stipulation is that the gift be beautifully wrapped and cost under $10.
- Everyone draws a number to select a gift.
- After all the gifts are selected, staff members may exchange their selection with other guests.

Initiate Peer Coaching

Goals

- Increase staff awareness of alternative forms of instruction.
- Enable staff to develop and maintain a high degree of collegiality.
- Empower staff to improve instruction from within their own ranks.
- Reward teacher leaders with meaningful staff development opportunities.

Links with Other ISLLC Standards

#1 Vision Values

#4 Community Connections

#5 Ethics Embodied

Resource

Robbins, P. (1991). *How to plan and implement a peer coaching program*. Association for Supervision and Curriculum Development.

Keep in Mind

- Introduce the concept of peer coaching to the staff through an in-service staff meeting.
- Support teacher leaders who wish to form a Critical Friends Group on a volunteer basis.
- Encourage teachers to attend professional development programs that emphasize alternative assessment methods.
- Ask other administrators to evaluate you using peer coaching techniques.

Develop a Character Education Program

Goals

- Create a safe environment for the entire school community.
- Reduce disciplinary referrals, suspensions, and expulsions.
- Lower dropout rates and increase academic achievement.

Links with Other ISLLC Standards

#1 Vision Values

#3 Safe and Sound

#4 Community Connections

#5 Ethics Embodied

#6 Politics, Please

Resource

C. Haynes, *Character Education Can Transform Students and Schools*. 1101 Wilson Blvd., Arlington, VA 22209: The Freedom Forum First Amendment Center., web site: www.freedomforum.org

Character Education Partnership

Web site: www.character.org

Phone: (800) 988-8081

Keep in Mind

- This a collaborative effort with staff, parents, students, and community involved in the design, implementation, and assessment.
- Character education programs thrive when they are expanded through the years.
- Media support is crucial to promote the school as a safe haven from violence.

Empower Teacher Experts

Goals

- Recognize and spotlight teacher leaders.
- Provide role models for staff and students in the area of instructional leadership.
- Encourage staff development in the area of technology.
- Role model effective peer coaching for all members of the school community.

Links with Other ISLLC Standards

#1 Vision Values   #5 Ethics Embodied

#4 Community Connections   #6 Politics, Please

Resource

Pam VanHorn, Principal
Kilbourne Middle School
50 E. Dublin-Granville Rd., Worthington, OH 43085
E-mail: pvanhorn@worthington.k12.oh.us

Keep in Mind

- Each staff member who has mastered an area of technology (i.e., web page design) teaches other interested adults in the building.
- Participants agree upon hours/days for in-service instruction.
- The instructor is readily available between arranged meeting times through online conversation and face-to-face meetings.
- If the instructor meets specific requirements, he or she may earn status as an adjunct professor at a nearby university or branch. By adding specific requirements, this professional development opportunity can become a course for graduate credit for those who choose to pay registration fees.

Showcase Skills in a Talent Show

Goals

- Draw the entire surrounding community into an evening of fun, entertainment, and learning.
- Help staff and students work together toward a positive goal.
- Keep mischief to a minimum at the end of the school year by focusing on this positive way to let off steam.
- Encourage contributions by all staff and students in nonperforming as well as performing areas.

Links with Other ISLLC Standards

#1 Vision Values

#3 Safe and Sound

#4 Community Connections

#6 Politics, Please

Resource

Pam VanHorn, Principal
Kilbourne Middle School
50 E. Dublin-Granville Rd., Worthington, OH 43085
E-mail: pvanhorn@worthington.k12.oh.us

Keep in Mind

- An end-of-the-year talent show provides the opportunity for students and staff members to showcase talent previously unseen by their middle school family.
- Only those who have a high quality performance to offer should be included in the show. An adult oversees practices, plans the order of the acts, and times them so the length of the program can be determined.
- Acts may include student-written skits, ballet, modern dance, step dancing, rock bands, poetry reading, violin, piano, voice solos, and much more.

Walk Down Memory Lane

Goals

- Highlight the traditions of the school through a visual history.
- Encourage alumni support of the school by including them in the culture of the current school operation.
- Encourage the feeling of school family with a pictorial history.
- Send the message that the school cares about students even after graduation.

Links with Other ISLLC Standards

#1 Vision Values

#3 Safe and Sound

#4 Community Connections

#5 Ethics Embodied

#6 Politics, Please

Resource

Dwight Carter, Assistant Principal
Gahanna-Lincoln High School
140 Hamilton Rd., Gahanna, OH 43230
E-mail: dwightc4@yahoo.com

Keep in Mind

- Make one area of the school a focal point for this project.
- Designate that area as a place where memorabilia from the past will be displayed.
- Encourage donations from the local historical society, alumni, and current students as possible display items.
- Refer to this area with pride as you address students, staff, and the community.

Hold a Brunch at Bob's

Goals

- Help build a strong culture within grade level teams.
- Reward students who go the extra mile in academics, volunteer work, or improved behavior.
- Make this special meal a time when students and teachers can communicate outside the usual school day schedule.

Links with Other ISLLC Standards

#1 Vision Values   #4 Community Connections

#3 Safe and Sound   #5 Ethics Embodied

Resource

Madeline Partlow, Principal
New Albany Middle School
6600 E. Dublin-Granville Rd., New Albany, OH 43054
E-mail: mpartlow@new-alban.k12.oh.us

Keep in Mind

- Each month, during the team planning time, each teacher picks one student to take to Bob Evans for a brunch.
- Each student who is picked is awarded a certificate that gives the reason he or she was chosen.
- While at brunch, the students tell who chose them and why.
- A member of the staff then lets the chosen students know that the teacher who chose them is watching for positive behavior during each day.
- This type of positive reinforcement of good behavior gives students an incentive to not only try to be chosen for Brunch at Bob's, but also makes them aware of what the expectations are for behavior and general attitude at that grade level.

Create Staff Technology Stations

Goals

- Encourage lifelong learning in the area of technology.
- Provide teachers with an informal, relaxed format in which to pursue technology training.
- Empower teachers to direct their own learning by asking them to select their own technology topics.
- Encourage the wider school district to become involved in technology training at your school.

Links with Other ISLLC Standards

#1 Vision Values

#4 Community Connections

#6 Politics, Please

Resource

Madeline Partlow, Principal
New Albany Middle School
6600 E. Dublin-Granville Rd., New Albany, OH 43054
E-mail: mpartlow@new-alban.k12.oh.us

Keep in Mind

- Teachers are surveyed regarding the types of technology they would be interested in learning more about.
- The top five technology topics chosen by staff are set up into stations during staff in-service days.
- Each station has instructions on a specific technology tool with assistance from the district's technology coordinator or an expert teacher. After 30 minutes at a station, the teacher/learner moves to another station.
- Some suggestions for the technology stations are digital camera use, Mind Manager, classroom portals, Excel, Inspiration, and I-Movie.

Give a "Dammit Doll"

Goals

- Recognize that stress and tension are a part of every educator's life.
- Give staff members tools to cope with stress.
- Add humor as a way to defuse tense situations in the workplace.

Links with Other ISLLC Standards

#1 Vision Values   #3 Safe and Sound

Resource

Amber C. Hejtmancik, School Psychologist
Gahanna-Jefferson Schools
160 South Hamilton Road
Gahanna, OH 43230
E-mail: hejtmancika@gjps.org
Dammit Doll pattern: Web site search words:
    Ages's Crochet Pages-Patterns-Dammit Doll

Keep in Mind

- This project can be used as a staff group activity, preferably in a retreat setting.
- Having many types of fabric and buttons available adds variety and flair to the creation of the dolls.
- If time is an issue, make sure that a sewing machine is available for use in putting the last stitches on the dolls.
- Having fun with this activity makes it a real team builder!

Schedule for Success

Goals

- Create a master schedule that is a powerful tool for fostering collegiality related to student learning.
- Set a tone for educational reform by building a master schedule that invites student learning.
- Keep disruptions to a minimum by maximizing the entire school day for learning.
- Send a message to the community that the master schedule's first priority is student achievement.

Links with Other ISLLC Standards

#1 Vision Values

#3 Safe and Sound

#4 Community Connections

#5 Politics, Please

Resource

James Grube, Principal
Westland High School
146 Galloway Rd., Galloway, OH 43119
E-mail: James_Grube@swcs.k12.oh.us

Keep in Mind

- Keep the number of class changes to a minimum.
- Together with teacher leaders, make site visits to schools to see the day-to-day operation of alternative schedules.
- Reduce study halls in order to decrease tardiness and discipline issues.
- Increase staff planning and development time.
- Implement lunch detentions in lieu of after-school detentions.

Personalize Each Child's Education

Goals

- Provide the opportunity for each child to have a trusted adult that they can talk to.
- Maximize learning by providing adult role models on a long-term basis.
- Decrease discipline issues by increasing the amount of adult-child interaction.

Links with Other ISLLC Standards

#1 Vision Values   #5 Ethics Embodied

#3 Safe and Sound

Resource

K. O'Neill, Connecting students with their school community. (Published by: Effective Schools, 2199 Jolly Road, Suite 160, Okemos, MI 48864.) *Research Abstracts, 2002-2003 Series,* 1(9).

Keep in Mind

- Provide multi-age classrooms where there is a spread of ages and a teacher follows students for more than one year.
- Establish looping, where a group of students advance together with the same teacher over a two- or three-year period.
- Restructure the school schedule and consider block scheduling so that teachers can get to know students more quickly.
- Provide adult, one-to-one mentoring for students who need extra help both academically and socially.
- Form advisory groups where a small group of students meets regularly with a teacher who acts as their advocate and advisor throughout their middle or high school years.

Accommodate All Learners
with Special Programs

Goals

- Reach all students by providing alternatives to the regular school day.
- Decrease dropout and truancy rates by seeking to find ways to engage students who do not respond to the traditional school day.
- Provide acceleration opportunities for students who have clear-cut career goals.

Links with Other ISLLC Standards

#1 Vision Values

#3 Safe and Sound

#4 Community Connections

Resource

Brice Frasure, Principal
Logan High School
50 North St.
Logan, OH 43138
E-mail: Bfrasure@loganhocking.k12.oh.us

Keep in Mind

- Design alternatives to the normal high school day such as work release programs, proficiency camps, alternative high schools, and evening school programs.
- Allow students to take extra courses during summer sessions.
- Encourage all students to graduate from high school by participating in alternative programs if desired.

Know That Trust Is a Must

Goals

- Establish a positive climate for student achievement by focusing on building professional trust.
- Gauge the climate of the school by providing informal opportunities for staff to relax and regroup.
- Set a tone of trust and decency for the whole school by developing good staff relations.

Links with Other ISLLC Standards

#1 Vision Values

#3 Safe and Sound

#4 Community Connections

#5 Ethics Embodied

#6 Politics, Please

Resource

James Grube, Principal
Westland High School
146 Galloway Rd.
Galloway, OH 43119
E-mail: James_Grube@swcs.k12.oh.us

Keep in Mind

- Plan an annual school retreat with your staff.
- Have an administration-sponsored cookout for the staff with administrators as chefs.
- Develop a catch phrase to rally around, such as "Expect Success."
- Keep staff informed of the Good, the Bad, and the Ugly.
- Have a tailgate party during lunch for staff on Football Fridays.

Encourage Service Learning Opportunities

Goals

- Help students recognize the value of volunteer work.
- Engage the school's commitment to community.
- Expand the traditional curriculum with hands-on experience.
- Publicize the school's commitment to the community.

Links with Other ISLLC Standards

#1 Vision Values   #5 Ethics Embodied

#3 Safe and Sound   #6 Politics, Please

#4 Community Connections

Resources

Keith Richards, Superintendent
Newark City Schools
85 E Main St.
Newark, OH 43055
Phone: (740) 345-9891

Keep in Mind

- Students can earn a service learning award each quarter by completing two hours of community service.
- The school provides various service activities on site, such as a blood drive, nursing home visitations, community dinners, Pancake Days, Relay for Life Support, and Operation Feed collection.
- There are also several after-school groups such as Builders' Club (youth extension of Kiwanis) and Youth-to-Youth (a drug-free program).
- Students can also earn service credits by working in their neighborhoods doing various approved projects.
- It is important to note that students do not get paid for work to be eligible to receive service credits.

3

Safe and Sound: ISLLC Standard 3

"A school administrator is an educational leader who promotes the success of all students by ensuring management of the organization, operations, and resources for a safe, efficient, and effective learning environment."

Establish a Nuts and Bolts Committee

Goals

- Receive staff input on the day-to-day operations of the building.
- Take a long-range view of how management strategies affect the overall operation of the school.
- Constantly tweak current policies and procedures as the school evolves in terms of outside political influences, local community changes, and safety considerations.

Links with Other ISLLC Standards

#1 Vision Values

#2 Culture Counts

#4 Community Connections

#6 Politics, Please

Resource

Dr. Richard Littell, Principal
Thomas Worthington High School
300 West Dublin-Granville Road
Worthington, OH 43085
E-mail: rlitell@worthington.k12.oh.us

Keep in Mind

- This is a voluntary committee comprised of staff members and administration who meet periodically to determine what's working and what's not working.
- Typical items include editing of the staff handbook, examination of the student code of conduct, and analysis of the daily operations of the building.
- Each department/team is encouraged to have at least one member serve on this committee.

Publish a Principal's Monthly Newsletter

Goals

- Ensure formalized communication with parents and community.
- Use the format as a community relations vehicle as well as an informational tool.
- Provide safety and security information as well as school events.
- Make communication of data a part of this effort.

Links with Other ISLLC Standards

#1 Vision Values   #4 Community Connections

#2 Culture Counts   #6 Politics, Please

Resource

Northwest Regional Educational Laboratory
101 SW Main St., Portland, OR 97204
Web site: ww.nwrel.orgu

Keep in Mind

- The No Child Left Behind Act provides that parents receive more information about their child's school. This not only includes information about individual progress but also more parent and community involvement. A monthly newsletter can give parents clear, concise, and readable information about the school.
- In addition to focusing on student activities, the newsletter can provide resource material to parents that deals with parent involvement, assesses family needs and interests about working with the school, fosters communication, and develops outreach programs relevant to the school community.
- The newsletter can initiate parent communication within the staff development program of the school.

Implement a Safe School Help Line

Goals

- Reassure the school and larger community that safety issues are addressed immediately.
- Provide school officials with information about potential safety challenges in the district.
- Keep an open line of communication between the school and the community.
- Address national and international security issues in the context of the safety of each child.

Links with Other ISLLC Standards

#1 Vision Values
#2 Culture Counts
#4 Community Connections
#6 Politics, Please

Resource

Security Voice Inc., Phone: (800) 325-4381
Website: www.schoolhelpline.com

Keep in Mind

- Many school districts have established hotlines or help lines for students, staff, and community members to anonymously leave information.
- One such hotline, the Safe School Help Line, gives each school a separate 800 number. When a call is received, the message is transcribed and sent to the school.
- The school can then decide what to do with the information. The caller is given an identification number if he or she wants to call back to see what action was taken.
- This Web site also provides a school safety questionnaire that administrators might find helpful in assessing the feelings of personal safety among students.

Fine Tune The School's Emergency Plan

Goals

- Comply with district-level emergency standards.
- Provide emergency procedures within the unique context of each school's needs.
- Stay on top of changing local, national, and international safety concerns.
- Provide timely information to the entire school community that safety is on the front burner of the principal's agenda.

Links with Other ISLLC Standards

#1 Vision Values   #5 Ethics Embodied

#2 Culture Counts   #6 Politics, Please

#4 Community Connections

Resources

Steve Mazzi, Principal
Big Walnut Middle School
105 Baughman St., PO Box 5002, Sunbury, OH 43074
E-mail: mazzi@bigwalnut.k12.oh.us

Your state's State Fire Marshal's Web site

Keep in Mind

- By law, school principals must establish, practice, and document all emergency procedures and drills in the building.
- All staff and students must receive the procedures in writing and be involved in drills.
- Recommendations from staff, students, and administrators should be welcomed and encouraged.
- All dates and times of emergency drills must be documented in writing.

Conduct Regular Classroom Visits

Goals

- Stay visible and engaged in the instructional aspect of the school.
- Check on the physical plant of the building during these visits.
- Send the message that the principal cares about the academic progress of each child.
- Make informal visits part of the "the way we do things around here."
- Provide an avenue for teachers and administrators to communicate informally about instruction.

Links with Other ISLLC Standards

#1 Vision Values

#2 Culture Counts

#4 Community Connections

#5 Ethics Embodied

Resource

Leading learning communities: Standards for what principals should know and be able to do. (2001). Alexandria, VA: The National Association of Elementary School Principals.

Keep in Mind

- As instructional leaders, principals need to stay in touch with what is going on in every classroom in the building.
- The goal is to spend at least 10 minutes in every classroom once every two weeks.
- A logbook of rooms visited will help ensure that all classes are regularly visited.

Incorporate a School Resource Officer

Goals

- Make sure local law enforcement is involved in the day-to-day-lives of students during school hours.
- Educate all students regarding the necessity for a safe and orderly environment.
- Inform the entire school community of local law enforcement services.

Link with Other ISLLC Standards

#1 Vision Values

#2 Culture Counts

#4 Community Connections

#5 Ethics Embodied

#6 Politics, Please

Resource

U.S. Department of Justice
Office of Community Oriented Policy Services
1100 Vermont Avenue NW
Washington, D.C. 20530
Web site: www.cops.usdoj.gov

Keep in Mind

- COPS (Community Oriented Policing Services in the Schools) is part of a federal grant program designed to introduce community policing into the schools by educating both law enforcement and school administrators in community policing training curriculum.
- The program is designed to provide resource information for administrators, teachers, and students in their efforts to provide safe schools.
- The program incorporates problem-based learning into its curriculum as a means of helping all involved retain information over a lifetime.

Start a Safe and Drug-Free Schools Program

Goals

- Involve the entire community in proactive planning regarding safety issues.
- Incorporate ethics into student learning.
- View the larger world in terms of each student's responsibility to contribute to a safe and sound building.

Links with Other ISLLC Standards

#1 Vision Values

#2 Culture Counts

#4 Community Connections

#5 Ethics Embodied

#6 Politics, Please

Resource

U.S. Department of Education
Office of Safe and Drug-Free Schools
News Branch
400 Maryland Avenue, SW
Washington, D. C. 20202
Phone: (202) 260-3943
Web site: www.governmentguide.com
Web site: www.cops.usdoj.gov

Keep in Mind

- Federal grants are available and are administered through states. Monies obtained can be used for drug prevention.
- A drug prevention program may include guest speakers and literature.
- This program can be implemented in conjunction with Character Education Programs.

Hire an Attendance Manager

Goals

- Improve attendance with the help of an administrative assistant.
- Assure that attendance is a top priority in the school environment.
- Focus on attendance by providing in-depth attention to this vital component of educational achievement.
- Provide a school liaison to local juvenile authorities.

Links with Other ISLLC Standards

#1 Vision Values
#2 Culture Counts
#4 Community Connections

Resource

Christine Cline, Staff Development Teacher
Richard Avenue Elementary School
3646 Richard Avenue
Grove City, OH 43123
E-mail: Christine_Cline@swcs.k12.oh.us

Keep in Mind

- The responsibility of the attendance manager is to track unaccounted absences.
- The attendance manager makes every attempt to find out where the absent child is and why. This can save the principal hours of time.
- The manager informs parents about procedures for truancy, up to and including legal action.
- This position is a valuable tool in elementary schools that do not have assistant principals on staff.

Don't Overlook Safe School Details

Goals

- Make sure all pieces of the puzzle fit together when designing safe school procedures.
- Provide easy-to-follow steps in case of emergencies.
- Minimize confusion when emergencies arise.

Links with Other ISLLC Standards:

#2 Culture Counts

#4 Community Connections

#6 Politics, Please

Resources

John Lanka, Principal
Monroe Elementary School
5000 St. Rt. 38
London, OH 43140
E-mail: lankaj@alder.
k12.oh.us43207

Chris Lester, Assistant
Superintendent
Hamilton Local Schools
4999 Lockbourne Rd.
Columbus, OH
E-mail: clester@mail.
hamilton-k12.oh.us

Keep in Mind

- Doors are secured so that entrance to the building can only be gained through the front door.
- A pressure mat is located inside the front door to notify office staff of anyone entering the building.
- Digital cameras are used to monitor hallways, entrances, playgrounds, and parking lots of school facilities.
- Playground area is secured by fencing to discourage visitors from entering through any way other than the front doors.
- Visitor sign-in and badge distribution are done at the main office so that the visitor is easily identifiable to all staff and students.
- A welcome desk is located inside the school's main entrance. It is staffed by a teacher or parent volunteer.

Implement a Freshman Connection Program

Goals

- Acclimate ninth graders into high school in an organized program.
- Promote vertical articulation opportunities between feeder middle school(s) and the receiving high school.
- Provide a smooth transition both academically and emotionally for entering freshmen.
- Help parents also make the transition from one school to another.

Links with Other ISLLC Standards

#1 Vision Values
#2 Culture Counts
#4 Community Connections
#5 Ethics Embodied

Resource

Dr. Richard Littell, Principal
Thomas Worthington High School
300 W Dublin-Granville Rd., Worthington, OH 43085
E-mail: rlittell@worthington.k12.oh.us

Keep in Mind

- This program begins in February with a Future Decisions Night at the school for 8th grade students and their parents.
- High school teachers then visit the middle school to discuss curriculum opportunities.
- In late spring, middle school students again return to the high school for tours led by high school students.
- During the summer, entering freshmen received their schedules, meet with their counselors, and attend an evening orientation.

Train Staff in Nonviolent Intervention

Goals

- Model nonviolent behavior for students by training staff in violence prevention techniques.
- Assure the community that students are being dealt with in a fair and equitable manner.

Links with Other ISLLC Standards

#1 Vision Values

#2 Culture Counts

#3 Community Connections

Resource

Mike Beck, Principal
Groveport Madison Freshman High School
751 E Main St.
Groveport, OH 43125
Phone: (614) 836-4957
Web site: crisisprevention.com

Keep in Mind

- The Nonviolent Crisis Prevention Program (CPI) has been successfully training individuals for over 20 years.
- Nonviolent intervention helps staff members restrain students who are out of control without risking injury to the student or the adult.
- If this program is implemented building-wide, it gives staff a plan to follow when dealing with rare situations of violence. It also ensures the safety of students.
- Inform parents of this program as an example of the school's belief in nonviolence.

Tame Difficult People

Goals

- Keep the focus on the vision of the school.
- Maintain a culture of dignity and respect.
- Serve as a role model for appropriate behavior to children.
- Provide community members with appropriate conflict resolution skills.

Links with Other ISLLC Standards

#1 Vision Values   #5 Ethics Embodied

#2 Culture Counts   #6 Politics, Please

#4 Community Connections

Resource

Ruth Kotler, Principal's licensure candidate
Ashland University, Columbus, Ohio
Unpublished paper, December 2003
E-mail: rkotler@columbus.rr.com

Keep in Mind

- Recognize that angry people are fearful people.
- Keep your jaw relaxed when difficult people are angry with you.
- Maintain neutrality in your eyes so fuel is not added to the fire.
- Make every attempt to listen sincerely.
- Increase your understanding by repeating, restating, paraphrasing, or summarizing major points of their statement.
- Explain your point of view using "I" statements.
- Look for areas of agreement. For example, state: "We both want Jordan to do well in school. How can we work together to ensure that it happens?"

Gain Knowledge of Physical Space Issues

Goals

- Be aware of cost-saving methods for use of the building facility.
- Become knowledgeable about creative ways to reconfigure existing physical space in order to accommodate upgrading curriculum.
- Understand that efficient use of space translates into community support for the school.
- Make sure individuals with physical disabilities have appropriate accommodations within the school setting.

Links with Other ISLLC Standards

#1 Vision Values   #5 Ethics Embodied

#2 Culture Counts   #6 Politics, Please

#4 Community Connections

Resource

Karl Martin, Superintendent
Athens City School District
25 S Plain Rd., The Plains, OH 45780-1340
Phone: (740) 797-4544

Keep in Mind

- Seek ideas about the best use of space from the school treasurer, district business manager, and superintendent as well as other principals.
- Communicate with the district architect and school facilities director about ways to reconfigure the existing building to meet people and curriculum needs.
- Use your state's elementary and secondary principal associations to expand your network of contacts in this area.

Establish Peer Dyads

Goals

- Increase standardized national and state test scores.
- Provide day-to-day academic help for students in need.
- Build tutoring opportunities into the master schedule.
- Establish one-to-one mentoring relationships between students.
- Provide gifted students with service learning opportunities.
- Affirm the school's vision with students at all achievement and behavioral levels.

Links with Other ISLLC Standards

#1 Vision Values   #4 Community Connections

#2 Culture Counts   #6 Politics, Please

Resource

American Institutes for Research
1000 Thomas Jefferson St., NW
Washington, D.C. 20007-3835
Web site: www.air.org

Keep in Mind

- Pairing students for academic tutoring provides opportunities to engage in oral reading and comprehension practice.
- Components of peer dyads include pair assignments, peer tutoring sessions three to four times per week, and error correction.
- Peer mentors can assist peers with classroom survival skills, social skills, and replacement behaviors for inappropriate interactions.
- The classroom teacher can provide parallel incentives for positive behavior by providing token systems to reinforce appropriate classroom behavior.

Remember: Followers Are Volunteers

Goals

- Build a network of collaborative leadership to implement the school's vision.
- Provide all members of the school community with a voice in the school's operation.
- Establish a tone of trust within the school community.

Links with Other ISLLC Standards

#1 Vision Values

#2 Culture Counts

#4 Community Connections

#5 Ethics Embodied

#6 Politics, Please

Resource

DuPree, M. (1992). *Leadership jazz*. New York, NY: Dell Publishing.

Keep in Mind

Expect these questions from followers:

- What may I expect from you?
- Can I achieve my own goals by following you?
- Will I reach my potential by working with you?
- Can I entrust my future to you?
- Have you bothered to prepare yourself for leadership?
- Are you ready to be ruthlessly honest?
- Do you have the self-confidence and trust to let me do my job?
- What do you believe?

Keep Interruptions to a Minimum

Goals

- Provide a smooth flow to the daily operations of the school.
- Keep instructional time to a maximum.
- Ensure that discipline issues are reduced by assisting teachers in their classroom management efforts.
- Set boundaries for the community in general when communicating with the school.
- Keep high-stakes testing in the forefront of the daily operation of the school.

Links with Other ISLLC Standards

#1 Vision Values   #5 Ethics Embodied

#2 Culture Counts   #6 Politics, Please

#4 Community Connections

Resource

Daniel Kinley, Principal
St. Matthias Elementary School
1566 Ferris Rd., Columbus, OH 43224
E-mail: dkinley@cdeducation.org

Keep in Mind

- Announcements on the building's intercom should be given at designated times only, such as after the morning bell and before the bell at the end of the day.
- A schoolwide announcement may be given at mid-day, prior to the lunch periods, to announce changes in schedule, such as indoor recess.
- Parents are to go directly to the office when picking up a student or dropping off materials for their child. The student will then be called to the office or will receive the materials at an appropriate time.

Establish the Position of Records Officer

Goals

- Make sure that all federal laws regarding student information are followed to the letter.
- Stay in compliance with district policy by building this position into an administrative assistant's job description.
- Protect student privacy by setting a tone of advocacy for students.

Links with Other ISLLC Standards

#2 Culture Counts

#4 Community Connections

#5 Ethics Embodied

#6 Politics, Please

Resource

DuFour, R., Burnette, R., & Eaker, R. E. (2002). *Getting started: Reculturing schools to become professional learning communities.* Bloomington, IN: National Educational Service.

Keep in Mind

- The person in this position knows how and where to file away student information on the computer or in a file cabinet.
- The Records Office is accountable for all student records within the building.
- Teachers and parents must use the Records Office to obtain student information.

Develop a Student Forum

Goals

- Give students a voice in the operation of the school.
- Establish a tone of trust with students.
- Keep the lines of communication open with students.
- Model respectful behavior for all generations to the entire community.
- Include service learning as a component of your professional mission.

Links with Other ISLLC Standards

#1 Vision Values

#2 Culture Counts

#4 Community Connections

#5 Ethics Embodied

#6 Politics, Please

Resource

Dr. Richard Littell, Principal
Thomas Worthington High School
300 West Dublin-Granville Rd., Worthington, OH 43085
E-mail: rlitell@worthington.k12.oh.us

Keep in Mind

- Student forums are regular meetings designed to bring the principal together with student leaders from the entire school.
- Student leaders may include student council members and officers, class officers, athletic team captains, and *any other students interested in participating.*
- Student forums provide a voice to diverse groups within the student body.
- Students discuss a variety of issues related to school policies and procedures, safety within the school, school climate and culture, and achievement.

Provide Social Skills Training

Goals

- Promote a tone of respectful behavior with students and staff.
- Provide opportunities to address problem areas in communication in a nonthreatening manner.
- Set an example of social skill literacy for staff and students.
- Provide opportunities for personal growth for everyone in the school community.
- Stress the importance of appropriate behavior to students as a lifelong learning process.

Links with Other ISLLC Standards

#1 Vision Values   #5 Ethics Embodied

#2 Culture Counts   #6 Politics, Please

#4 Community Connections

Resource

McGinnis, Dr. E., & Goldstein, Dr. A. P. (2000). *Skillstreaming the elementary child: New strategies and perspectives for teaching prosocial skills*. Research Press.

Keep in Mind

- The entire school can participate in social skills training.
- Teachers and staff learn about teaching students social skills with lessons provided in the book.
- Offer school assemblies that focus on a skill such as listening.
- Skills are practiced in the classroom. When "caught" doing a skill that is the current focus, students earn tickets for a weekly drawing.

Design a Substitute Teacher Booklet

Goals

- Educate substitute teachers about the daily operation of the building.
- Provide a welcoming climate for substitute teachers.
- Ensure schoolwide safety issues are followed by all personnel.
- Provide classroom management support for substitute teachers.

Links with Other ISLLC Standards

#1 Vision Values

#2 Culture Counts

#4 Community Connections

Resource

Michelle Manley, Literacy Support Teacher
Oak Creek Elementary School
1256 Westwood Dr.
Lewis Center, OH 43035
E-mail: michelle_manley@olentangy.k12.oh.us

Keep in Mind

- Substitute teachers are an integral part of the school community.
- It helps the entire daily operation of the school to nurture, support, and inform substitute teachers of school operations.
- Students perform at a higher level of achievement when they know that support is provided for substitute teachers from the school administration.
- Substitute teachers will return again and again to schools that provide them with the necessary tools to effectively manage the school day.

4

Community Connections: ISLLC Standard 4

"A school administrator is an educational leader who promotes the success of all students by collaborating with families and community members, responding to diverse community interests and needs and mobilizing community resources."

Develop Unity Day

Goals

- Plan an appropriate memorial to 9/11 in which the entire community can participate.
- Set the tone for how students should conduct themselves during a solemn occasion.
- Establish a tradition that will tie into the school's vision and culture.

Links with Other ISLLC Standards

#1 Vision Values
#2 Culture Counts
#5 Ethics Embodied
#6 Politics, Please

Resources

Dr. Gail Mitchell, Principal
Moler Elementary School
1560 Moler Rd., Columbus, OH 43207
Phone: (614) 365-5529

Keep in Mind

- In remembrance of 9/11, community members, armed forces personnel, and various public servants are invited to the school.
- Speeches are given to promote unity by all generations, including students.
- Acts of unity are displayed by students in the form of artwork, plays, musical selections, and poetry readings.
- Armed services veterans from the community who never received their high school diplomas (from World War II through the Gulf War) are awarded honorary high school diplomas.
- Invited speakers give motivational talks.

Host a Meet the Candidates Night

Goals

- Provide a forum for discussion of political issues and candidates within the school community.
- Help parents teach their children about local issues of concern.
- Engage local politicians in the school community.

Links with Other ISLLC Standards

#1 Vision Values

#2 Culture Counts

#5 Ethics Embodied

#6 Politics, Please

Resource

Ron Hairston, Principal
Sunshine Christian Academy
2112 Mock Rd.
Columbus, OH 43219
Phone: (614) 475-7887

Keep in Mind

- Before an election, invite candidates to your school to meet parents and students.
- Give the candidates a forum to discuss their positions on issues, and provide an opportunity to discuss those issues.
- Allow parents to question candidates without input from the media.
- As an incentive, the class with the largest parental representation receives a pizza party.

Initiate an "Adopt a Community Leader" Campaign

Goals

- Ensure that students become participants in the community's political process.
- Provide role models for future careers in public service, business, clergy, and nonprofit organizations.
- Network with community stakeholders to ensure sound communication between the school and the wider world.
- Expose students to a broad spectrum of leaders.

Links with Other ISLLC Standards

#1 Vision Values

#2 Culture Counts

#3 Safe and Sound

#6 Politics, Please

Resource

Ron Hairston, Principal
Sunshine Christian Academy
2112 Mock Rd., Columbus, OH 43219
Phone: (614) 475-7887

Keep in Mind

- Ask each class to adopt a community leader.
- Have students write letters to the individual describing themselves and their school and request correspondence.
- Invite "adoptees" to the school for a presentation.
- Make this a special day by having students greet leaders at the door, providing snacks, and encouraging a question-answer session with the community leaders.

Incorporate an "I Know I Can" Program

Goals

- Encourage urban students to seek the avenue of higher education.
- Keep an open door policy with community resources.
- Encourage business/school partnerships in the development of strong community leaders.
- Encourage volunteerism in young adults.

Links with Other ISLLC Standards

#1 Vision Values	#5 Ethics Embodied
#2 Culture Counts	#6 Politics, Please

Resource

Eddie Harrell Jr., Executive Director
I Know I Can Program
270 East State St., Columbus, OH 43215
Phone: (614) 469-7044
Web site: www.iknowican.org

Keep in Mind

- This nonprofit organization gives every qualified graduate the chance to succeed by assuring them the opportunity to go to college.
- The program, created in 1988, resulted when business and community leaders recognized that educated citizens are the foundation of a growing city and a prosperous economy.
- The program is meant to motivate students to stay in school, assist students who plan to pursue college, provide counseling, and award Last Dollar Grant assistance to qualified students.
- Recipients of these grants are required to volunteer their services to the community for each grant received.

Initiate a Partnership with Senior Citizens

Goals

- Provide a way to begin mentoring relationships between senior citizens and students.
- Focus the school community on the many contributions that senior citizens have made.
- Bridge the generation gap by allowing senior citizens and students to meet and converse in an informal atmosphere.
- Encourage senior citizens to participate in the day-to-day activities of the school community.

Links with Other ISLLC Standards

#1 Vision Values
#2 Culture Counts
#5 Ethics Embodied
#6 Politics, Please

Resource

Bob Britton, Principal
Elgin High School
1239 Keener Rd. South, Marion, OH 43302
E-mail: britton_b@treca.org

Keep in Mind

- This program is often developed by English and drama departments.
- Students phone senior citizens in the community who have made an impact in society or the neighborhood. Interview questions are prepared in advance by students.
- A drama class uses the interviews to construct a short play or skit to show during an assembly that is open to the community.
- Senior citizens are invited as the guests of honor.

Begin the School Year
with a Neighborhood Walk or Bus Trip

Goals

- Provide an informal avenue for neighborhood residents to communicate with school personnel.
- Assist new and veteran staff members in understanding the socioeconomic range in the neighborhood that the school serves.
- Use a forum to begin a conversation with faculty about how to best serve the needs of students.

Links with Other ISLLC Standards

#1 Vision Value

#2 Culture Counts

#3 Safe and Sound

#5 Ethics Embodied

#6 Politics, Please

Resource

Richard H. Vance, Principal
West Broad Elementary School
2744 W Broad St., Columbus, OH 43204
Phone: (614) 365-5964

Keep in Mind

- Prior to the first day of school, teachers, support staff, and administrators take a walk or ride though the neighborhood.
- Stops are made along the way so that staff can personally introduce themselves to parents, students, and community members.
- This personal touch can help break the ice at the beginning of the school year as the school reaches out in a very real way to the community.

Offer Parent Enrichment Classes

Goals

- Assist parents in lifelong learning.
- Show students that adults as well as children are learners.
- Provide extended use of the school building into the evening hours.
- Provide school personnel with an opportunity to interact with parents outside the framework of student progress.

Links with Other ISLLC Standards

#1 Vision Values
#2 Culture Counts
#3 Safe and Sound
#6 Politics, Please

Resource

National PTA
330 N. Wabash Ave.
Chicago, IL 60611
Phone: (312) 670-6782
Web site: www.pta.org/parentinvolvement

Keep in Mind

- Parenting classes or enrichment opportunities at the school promote community involvement.
- Classes taught can be determined by a needs survey sent to parents.
- Community volunteers may be available to teach the classes.
- Possible options for classes include cake decorating, keyboarding, yoga, and aerobics.

Start a Visible Woman Club

Goals

- Help teenage girls make the transition into adulthood in a supportive atmosphere.
- Call attention to the school's commitment to diversity issues.
- Promote better understanding of gender differences and roles to the entire school community.

Links with Other ISLLC Standards

#1 Value Vision
#2 Culture Counts
#3 Safe and Sound
#5 Ethics Embodied
#6 Politics, Please

Resource

Educational Technology Training Center
Web site: www.ettc.net/bestpractices
Cranford High School
105 West End Place
Cranford, NJ 07016
Phone: (908) 272-9100

Keep in Mind

- Female high school students meet biweekly to discuss the concerns of growing up female. They hold brunches to aid battered women. Women of achievement in the community are invited as speakers.
- Students design and maintain their own Web site.
- During Women's History Month, a schoolwide forum is held on a relevant feminist topic (eating disorders, depression, school bias, achievement gaps in math and science).

Open the School's Computer Lab to the Community

Goals

- Educate the entire community about the latest in computer technology.
- Engage the community in the learning process.
- Make use of extended hours for good use of the school building.
- Provide adult as well as student learning.

Links with Other ISLLC Standards

#1 Vision Values
#2 Culture Counts
#3 Safe and Sound
#6 Politics, Please

Resource

Suellen Fitzwater, Principal
Etna Road Elementary School
4531 Etna Rd., Whitehall, OH 43123
E-mail: sfitzwater@whitehall.k12.oh.us

Keep in Mind

- One evening per month, the school's computer lab is open to any member of the community.
- Community members have access to computers with Internet capabilities, a scanner, and two color printers.
- Children under 12 must be accompanied by an adult.
- One member of the district's technology support staff stays to provide technical assistance or instruction to anyone who needs it. The principal is also present.
- This event is advertised in both the school newsletter and the local community newspaper.

Host Proficiency After Dark Program

Goals

- Provide schoolwide focus on academic achievement.
- Engagetheentire community in helping students improve standardized test scores.
- Raise the awareness level of all community members about the importance of statewide mandated testing.
- Utilize the school after-hours.

Links with Other ISLLC Standards

#1 Vision Values
#2 Culture Counts
#3 Safe and Sound
#6 Politics, Please

Resources

National Network
    of Partnership Schools
Johns Hopkins University
3003 N Charles St.
Suite 200
Baltimore, MD 21218

Kennedy Jr. High School
Cleveland, OH
Sophronia Hairston
Action Team Chair
Phone: (216) 921-1450
Web site:
www.csos.jhu.edu

Keep in Mind

- On the Friday night before the Ohio Proficiency Test, students stay overnight at school to participate in a preparation program led by teachers.
- Teachers provide tutoring in the five academic areas of the test.
- Counselors, community and local church members, parents, and custodial and security staff assist with sports, exercise, rest breaks, Friday night dinner, and Saturday morning breakfast.

Establish Action Teams for Partnerships

Goals

- Provide teacher leadership in the area of community engagement.
- Bring community involvement into the forefront of the school's vision.
- Help establish a central location that community members can access with ideas and questions.
- Integrate all curricular areas in the practical application of community networking.

Links with Other ISLLC Standards

#1 Vision Values   #6 Politics, Please

#2 Culture Counts

Resource

National Network of Partnership Schools
Johns Hopkins University
3003 N Charles St., Suite 200, Baltimore, MD 21218
Web site: www.csos.jhu.edu

Keep in Mind

- The action team is responsible for assessing present partnership practices for community involvement. The team writes plans, implements activities, and evaluates coordination of practices for involvement between school, family, and community.
- Team members include two to three teachers from different grade levels, a parent liaison, one administrator, one member of the community, and two students from different grade levels. A cafeteria worker, school nurse, or a counselor may also be included on the action team.
- Diversity among members of the action team ensures activities will address the needs, interests, and talents of the entire school community.

Serve Breakfast on the Run

Goals

- Provide volunteer opportunities for students within the framework of the school day.
- Help busy parents connect with the school in an informal manner.
- Show appreciation to parents for supporting their child's school.

Links with Other ISLLC Standards

#1 Vision Values
#2 Culture Counts

Reference

National PTA
330 N Wabash Ave.
Chicago, IL 60611
Phone: (312) 670-6782
Web site: www.pta.org/parentinvolvement

Keep in Mind

- This program can be done by grade level or with different grade level teams working cooperatively with one another.
- Working parents are invited to the school one day per month.
- Students host a "curbside" breakfast for parents, including doughnuts, fruit, coffee, and juice.
- Students can buy their parents gift certificates in advance to redeem on the morning of the breakfast.

Hold a Rise and Shine Assembly

Goals

- Help students develop public speaking skills.
- Involve parents and community members in a friendly start of the day.
- Increase community involvement in the school in an informal manner.

Links with Other ISLLC Standards

#1 Vision Values

#2 Culture Counts

#3 Safe and Sound

#6 Politics, Please

Resource

The Principal Files
Web site: www.educationworld.com

Keep in Mind

- This is a great way to showcase student learning through public speaking.
- Parents and community members are invited to the school on a Friday morning.
- The school spotlights a different grade level or team at each assembly.
- Every student in the class gets an opportunity to shine at the microphone by speaking to the crowd.
- This assembly can be held several times a year or each week.

Design a Grandpersons' Day

Goals

- Increase involvement of "grandpersons" in the school.
- Honor the World War II generation with a creative performance by students.
- Send a message to the larger community that your school supports intergenerational enrichment activities.

Links with Other ISLLC Standards

#1 Vision Values
#2 Culture Counts
#5 Ethics Embodied
#6 Politics, Please

Resource

The Principal Files
Web site: www.educationworld.com

Keep in Mind

- A Grandpersons' Day is held on the Friday before Mother's Day.
- A grandperson in a child's life (not necessarily a *grandparent*) attends a special performance and goes to the student's classroom to work on a project.
- The grandperson accompanies the child to lunch and recess.
- A USO show can be held as a culminating activity related to the study of World War II for this special day.

Create a Principal for a Day Program

Goals

- Provide community leaders with hands-on experience in schools.
- Serve as a public relations vehicle to bring the school's mission to community stakeholders.

Links with Other ISLLC Standards

#1 Vision Values
#2 Culture Counts
#5 Ethics Embodied
#6 Politics, Please

Resource

Krista Morelli, Office of Development
Columbus Public Schools
270 E State St., Columbus, OH 43215
E-mail: kmorelli@columbus.k12.oh.us

Keep in Mind

- Business leaders and CEOs in geographic areas surrounding each school spend a day in the schools to solidify the number of partnerships between schools and the business community.
- Suggested activities for the business leaders are:
  - Leading classroom discussions
  - Reading to students
  - Teaching a "mini" lesson
  - Tutoring
  - Meeting with representatives from parent groups
  - Attending special assemblies/performances
  - Meeting with student council or other student leadership groups
- Encourage the media to become involved in this activity.

Design a Community "Litter-Acy" Program

Goals

- Teach students about the importance of a clean environment.
- Engage community leaders in a hands-on school project.
- Develop student contacts with future mentors.
- Provide community service within the framework of the school curriculum.

Links with Other ISLLC Standards

#1 Vision Values
#5 Ethics Embodied
#6 Politics, Please

Resource

The Bush School
3400 E Harrison St.
Seattle, WA 98112
Web site: www.bush.edu

Keep in Mind

- Community leaders come to school to discuss litter in the local community with students.
- Together, community leaders and students create a litter patrol for the school grounds.
- Community helpers assist students in the collection, chart the time it takes to clean the school grounds and sort the trash, and discuss recycling.
- Students establish a recycling program to help keep school grounds clean.

Create a Community Garden

Goals

- Teach students about the importance of the environment through this hands-on project.
- Give students an opportunity to participate in a service project.
- Connect the larger community to the everyday life of the school.

Links with Other ISLLC Standards

#1 Vision Values

#2 Culture Counts

#3 Safe and Sound

#5 Ethics Embodied

#6 Politics, Please

Resource

City Farmer, Canada's Office of Urban Agriculture
801-318 Homer St., Vancouver, BC. V68 2V3
Phone: (664) 685-5832
Web site: www.cityfarmer.org

Keep in Mind

- Designate an area around the schoolyard to be used for the garden.
- Permit parents and community members to educate each class about life sciences as well as standards-based teaching from classroom teachers.
- Make a school garden consisting of native plants and flowers.
- Create a schedule for upkeep of the garden. Community members, students, and teachers are responsible for the maintenance.

Set Up a "Read to Me Mondays" Program

Goals

- Invite community members into the classroom on a regular basis.
- Establish mentoring relationships between community members and students.
- Encourage partnerships between the school and community businesses.

Links with Other ISLLC Standards

#1 Vision Values

#2 Culture Counts

#3 Safe and Sound

#5 Ethics Embodied

#6 Politics, Please

Resource

Beverly Downing, Principal
Indian Trail Elementary School
6767 Gender Rd.
Canal Winchester, OH 43110
Phone: (614) 833-2153

Keep in Mind

- Community members assist in literacy by:
  - Community members reading to students.
  - Students reading to community members.
- School secretaries set up a schedule as community members commit to a series of visits.
- Teachers plan for community members to participate in the classroom on the same schedule for the entire school, such as each Monday from 10–10:30 a.m.

Educate the Community about Special Needs

Goals

- Provide valuable information to the community about disabled individuals.
- Teach tolerance to students and the community.
- Help disabled students become an integral part of the community.
- Raise the awareness level of students, parents, teachers, and other community members about the specific needs of all children.

Links with Other ISLLC Standards

#1 Vision Values   #5 Ethics Embodied
#2 Culture Counts   #6 Politics, Please
#3 Safe and Sound

Resource

University of Missouri at Kansas City
Institute for Human Development
Carl F. Calkins, Ph.D., Director
E-mail: calkinsc@umkc.edu
Web site: www.ihd.umkc.edu

Keep in Mind

- The arts are used as a method to overcome negative stigmas associated with different disabilities.
- The school hosts drama programs focusing on the needs of people with disabilities.
- The disabilities focused on are seen in the school and the larger community.
- Performers of dramas are usually high school students, and often include student cast members with developmental disabilities
- Families and community are involved in the production and direction of the drama performances.

Incorporate a Proficiency Test Promise

Goals

- Provide school-parent communication about high-stakes testing.
- Set a tone of collaboration between the school and parents.
- Teach effective parenting skills in relation to standardized testing.
- Provide a feeling of trust and safety to students in the form of a wide support system.

Links with Other ISLLC Standards

#1 Vision Values   #5 Ethics Embodied

#2 Culture Counts   #6 Politics, Please

#3 Safe and Sound

Resource

Ralph Collins, Principal
Genoa Middle School
5948 Old 3-C Highway, Westerville, OH 43081
E-mail: collinsr@wcsoh.org

Keep in Mind

- Send a letter home to parents at the beginning of the school year, explaining the school's desire to provide a unified effort between home and the community in relation to proficiency testing.
- The letter explains how the school will be providing extra help and also notes contributions that parents can make at home each day throughout the year. Special suggestions are given for testing days.
- Have all involved (teacher, student, and parent/guardian) sign a promise to work together to increase learning and to better prepare for proficiency tests.

5

Ethics Embodied: ISLLC Standard 5

"A school administrator is an educational leader who promotes the success of all students by acting with integrity, fairness, and in an ethical manner."

Establish a Staff Ethics Council

Goals

- Provide a forum for discussion of the school's vision statement.
- Empower faculty to examine the day-to-day operations of the school in the context of ethics.
- Monitor ethical issues within the school community.
- Make sure the school is up-to-date on national and international ethics issues.

Links with Other ISLLC Standards

#1 Vision Values

#2 Culture Counts

#3 Safe and Sound

#4 Community Connections

#6 Politics, Please

Resource

Mindy Farry, Principal
Olentangy High School
675 Lewis Center Rd., Lewis Center, OH 43035
E-mail: Melinda_f@treca.org

Keep in Mind

- The Ethics Advisory Council is designed to keep up with the needs of faculty and staff.
- The Council consists of volunteers from different departments and varying levels of experience.
- The council regularly e-mails requests about concerns that need to be addressed to facilitate maximum learning for students.
- This concept also helps the principal keep lines of communication open regarding equitable staff scheduling and duty procedures.

Communicate Curriculum Standards to Parents

Goals

- Showcase the school to the public by establishing a commitment of adherence to state curriculum standards.
- Keep parents informed of ongoing developments in their child's curriculum needs.
- Provide an opportunity for the staff to work as a team in interpreting standards to the public.

Links with Other ISLLC Standards

#1 Vision Values

#2 Culture Counts

#4 Community Connections

#6 Politics, Please

Resource

Collaborative Communication Group
1801 Connecticut Ave. NW
Third Floor
Washington, D.C. 20009
Phone: (202) 986-4959
Web site: www.publicengagment.com

Keep in Mind

- This is an evening event designed to inform parents and the community on state curriculum standards.
- By educating parents on curriculum standards, parents can support both their children and the school.
- Building partnerships based upon collaboration helps in gaining trust between the community and the school.

Manage by Walking Around

Goals

- Establish visibility to the entire school community.
- Send a message that school is a safe place to be.
- Keep communication open among staff and students.
- Promote a feeling of trust toward the school administration in the llarger community.

Links with Other ISLLC Standards

#1 Vision Values
#2 Culture Counts
#3 Safe and Sound
#4 Community Connections
#6 Politics, Please

Resource

Dr. Sylvester Small, Superintendent
Akron Public Schools
70 N Broadway, Akron, OH 44308
E-mail: ssmall@akron.k12.oh.us

Keep in Mind

- This seemingly simple act can be perceived by staff, students, and the larger community as a sign of personal and professional commitment by the principal.
- The high visibility of the principal is a powerful deterrent to discipline issues within the school.
- For schools that are located in high crime neighborhoods, the feeling of physical and emotional safety that this activity produces can be invaluable in helping students achieve.
- By the same token, the "heard but never seen" principal can be viewed as disinterested in the welfare of the school.

Educate Staff about E-mail Communications

Goals

- Promote the ethical and legal issues of e-mail usage as well as its convenience.
- Help staff initiate dialogue on appropriate and inappropriate e-mail usage within the framework of the school day.
- Enlighten staff on confidentiality issues surrounding e-mail and the concept that there is no right of privacy regarding e-mail.

Links with Other ISLLC Standards

#1 Vision Values   #4 Community Connections
#2 Culture Counts   #6 Politics, Please
#3 Safe and Sound

Resource

Richard L. Mann, State Counsel
% The Ohio Association of Secondary School
    Administrators
8050 N High Street, Suite 180, Columbus, OH 43235-6484
Web site: www.oassa.org

Keep in Mind

- Case law has established that e-mail communications, just like office memos, fall within the broad definition of records subject to the inspection of the public.
- All employees should remember to use the same discretion with e-mail that they are expected to use in any written communication.
- Attorneys now have access to software search programs that can search through many e-mails, looking for a name, date, incident, or any other identifying information and retrieve the entire e-mail.

Be Aware of School Web Page Issues

Goals

- Educate all administrators and teachers on the importance of maintaining the school web page in a regulated manner.
- Prevent misuse of the web page by establishing its design and update it as part of the school's curriculum.
- Make sure copyright laws are upheld on the web page.

Links with Other ISLLC Standards

#1 Vision Values

#2 Culture Counts

#3 Safe and Sound

#4 Community Connections

#6 Politics, Please

Resource

Richard L. Mann, State Counsel

% The Ohio Association of Secondary School
    Administrators

8050 N High Street, Suite 180, Columbus, OH 43235-6484

Web site: www.oassa.org

Keep in Mind

- To monitor appropriate content, the ultimate responsibility for the Web site must remain with teachers and administrators.
- It is recommended that schools that develops web pages create a policy with guidelines for editing and adding content to the web page.
- These guidelines could be very similar to the guidelines for the student newspaper.
- The principal should have final approval of any information included in the web page.

Hold a Preseason Parent Meeting

Goals

- Communicate with parents the need for all adults to be on the same page regarding the responsibilities of student athletes.
- Reach out to the community in an effort to publicize the school's desire to uphold ethical and legal standards for athletes.
- Create a dialogue with all stakeholders engaged in the process of coaching student athletes.

Links with Other ISLLC Standards

#1 Vision Values
#2 Culture Counts
#3 Safe and Sound
#4 Community Connections
#6 Politics, Please

Resource

Jay Wolfe, High School Athletic Director
Olentangy High School
675 Lewis Center Rd.
Lewis Center, OH 43035
Phone: (740) 657-4100

Keep in Mind

- Before the beginning of each sport's individual season, coaches have a meeting with parents of athletes to discuss the upcoming season.
- Coaches explain the school's expectations regarding athletes' behavior on and off the playing field. In addition, new policies are outlined for the parents.
- At the end of the meeting, the athletic director opens the floor for questions from parents.

Initiate SMART Goals

Goals

- Engage entire staff in an adult learning activity.
- Serve as a model for lifelong learning to the entire school community.
- Focus on teachers' views of themselves as professionals.
- Keep student achievement in mind as a daily and yearly goal for all faculty.

Links with Other ISLLC Standards

#1 Vision Values
#2 Culture Counts
#4 Community Connections
#6 Politics, Please

Resources

DuFour, R., & DuFour, R. Professional learning communities online course. National Educational Service, web site: www.nesonline.com

Mindy Farry, Principal, Olentangy High School
675 Lewis Center Rd., Lewis Center, OH 43035
E-mail: Melinda_f@treca.org

Keep in Mind

- SMART goals (**S**pecific, **M**easurable, **A**ttainable, **R**easonable, **T**imely) are designed to help staff designate schoolwide target goals for the school year.
- All staff members select three goals: one for the classroom, one for professional development, and one for student achievement.
- To set the tone, the principal communicates his or her SMART goals for the year.

Help Staff Self-Evaluate

Goals

- Engage entire staff in an adult learning activity.
- Serve as a model for lifelong learning to the entire school community.
- Focus on teachers' views of themselves as professionals.
- Keep student achievement in mind as a daily as well as yearly goal for all faculty.

Links with Other ISLLC Standards

#1 Vision Values #4 Community Connections

#2 Culture Counts #6 Politics, Please

Resource

Barbara Blake, Principal
K-5 Grade Levels, Weinland Park Elementary School
211 W 7th Ave., Columbus, OH 43201
Phone: (614) 365-5903

Keep in Mind

- At the beginning of the school year, a self-evaluation form is given to all staff members.
- On the form, each staff member writes one personal goal for his or her classroom and one professional goal.
- A personal goal for a third grade math classroom may be: "Students will be able to independently make up their own word problems using any operation."
- A professional goal for the teacher might be: "Attend two differentiated learning seminars during the year."
- In January, the principal meets with each teacher to discuss progress on the goals.

Start the Day Right
with an Opening Ceremony

Goals

- Set the tone for focusing on learning during the school day.
- Get the day started on a positive note of community.
- Refocus on the vision of the school.
- Help the school culture maintain an atmosphere of reaching for student achievement.

Links with Other ISLLC Standards

#1 Vision Values	#3 Safe and Sound
#2 Culture Counts	#4 Community Connections

Resource

Stan Embry, Principal
Africentric Program at Mohawk Elementary School
300 E Livingston Ave., Columbus, OH 43215
Phone: (614) 365-6517

Keep in Mind

- Opening ceremony begins at 9 a.m. daily. Students enter the auditorium after eating breakfast.
- The ceremony lasts 15 minutes.
- The students first do a libation ceremony, where they honor ancestors from the past. Two students pour water from a wooden vessel into a plant.
- All students hold hands and sing the Negro National Anthem and then sign their school song.
- Students say the school pledge and recite "I Am a Genius" poem.
- The principal goes over a word of the week with the students.
- Announcements are made and students are dismissed with their teachers, who take them to class.

Be Sure to Delegate Responsibility

Goals

- Empower staff to become teacher leaders.
- Set the tone for team building for the entire school community.
- Provide more time for the principal to focus on instructional leadership.

Links with Other ISLLC Standards

#1 Culture Counts

#2 Vision Values

#4 Community Connections

Resource

Deborah Kozlesky, Principal
Cherrington Elementary School
522 Cherrington Rd.
Westerville, OH 43081
E-mail: kozlesd@wcsoh.org

Keep in Mind

- Triage the tasks that have to be accomplished.
- Involve the staff in decision making as much as possible.
- Establish teams to assume reasonable responsibilities to ensure all tasks are complete.
- Include leadership teams, intervention teams, and volunteer teams.

Do an Ethics Check

Goals

- Help the principal look at all sides of tough decisions.
- Provide an ethical framework to live by.
- Model ethical behavior for the school community.

Links with Other ISLLC Standards

#1 Vision Values

#2 Culture Counts

#3 Safe and Sound

#4 Community Connections

#6 Politics, Please

Resource

Blanchard, K., & Peale, N. V. (1988). *The power of ethical management* (p. 27). New York: William Morrow.

Keep in Mind

Ask yourself these questions when faced with a tough decision:

- Is it legal? Will I be violating either civil law or company policy?
- Is it balanced? Is it fair to all concerned in the short term as well as the long term? Does it promote win-win relationships?
- How will it make me feel about myself? Will it make me proud?
- Would I feel good if my decision were published in the newspaper? Would I feel good if my family knew about it?

Create Your Own Personal Mission Statement

Goals

- Help new and experienced principals clarify their personal goals in relation to their professional lives.
- Serve as a reality check when job responsibilities get extremely hectic.
- Help administrators develop a long-term personal and professional plan.

Links with Other ISLLC Standards

#1 Vision Values
#2 Culture Counts
#4 Community Connection
#6 Politics, Please

Resource

Dr. Sherry Lahr, Associate/Adjunct Professor
Ashland University
Columbus Center
1900 E. Dublin-Granville Rd.
Columbus, OH 43229
E-mail: slahr@netwalk.com

Keep in Mind

- Over a period of time, write down the things in your life that matter to you most.
- Ask yourself this question: What would I die for?
- Write a brief personal mission statement and place it in your office so that you will see it each day.
- Your personal mission statement may change over time. Keep that idea in mind as you work to balance your career and personal life.

Check Out the School's Budget

Goals

- Get an overview of what the school considers to be its most important financial priorities.
- Compare financial priorities with the best way to utilize monies in alignment with student achievement.
- Develop a long-term plan of priorities based on information learned from studying the budget.

Links with Other ISLLC Standards

#1 Vision Values

#2 Culture Counts

#3 Safe and Sound

#4 Community Connections

#6 Politics, Please

Resource:

Hackmann, D. G., Scmitt-Oliver, D. M., & Tracy, J. C. (2002). *The standards-based administrative internship: Putting the ISLLC Standards into practice*. Lanham, MD: Scarecrow Press, Inc.

Keep in Mind

- To ensure equity in the school budget, examine the monies allocated to all sports and extracurricular activities.
- Compare those figures with what is spent on academics.
- Discuss your findings with the school/district treasurer.

Find a Mentor Outside Your School District

Goals

- Seek a balanced view of professional issues from an administrator outside the culture of your current job.
- Establish a life outside your current work arena by seeking collegial support.
- Plan for your career over the long term with fellow colleagues from different areas of the state/country.

Links with Other ISLLC Standards

#1 Vision Values

#2 Culture Counts

#3 Safe and Sound

#4 Community Connections

#6 Politics, Please

Resource

Steven E. Raines, Executive Director
The Ohio Association of Secondary School Administrators
8050 N High Street, Suite 180
Columbus, OH 43235-6484
Web site: www.oassa.org

Keep in Mind

- Most states require that beginning administrators have a mentor within the school district.
- However, it is important to note that a more dispassionate view of professional issues can be obtained from administrators not caught up in the day-to-day stress of one particular school system.
- By seeking a trusted colleague through state professional organization contacts, a positive two-way support system can develop.

Know Your School District's Policies

Goals

- Be aware of legal and ethical issues that crop up on the job by familiarizing yourself with district policies and procedures.
- Determine the best way to handle "hot topics" by being well-versed in the district's view of those topics.

Links with Other ISLLC Standards

#1 Vision Values

#2 Culture Counts

#3 Safe and Sound

#4 Community Connections

#6 Politics, Please

Resource

William Whitlatch, Assistant Principal
Canal Winchester Intermediate School
122 Washington St.
Canal Winchester, OH 43110
E-mail: wwhitlat@canalwin.k12.oh.us

Keep in Mind

- Immediately after being appointed to an administrative position, read the policies and procedures manual for your school district.
- Refer to this manual often and be sure to keep it updated when new policies are established and old ones modified.
- Consult on a routine basis with veteran administrators in the district regarding their interpretation of policies and procedures.

Remember: You May Not Always Have to Act!

Goals

- Learn that the principal does not have to solve every problem.
- Controlling all issues in the school is an impossibility.
- Empower staff to be in charge of finding solutions to day-to-day challenges.

Links with Other ISLLC Standards

#1 Vision Values

#2 Culture Counts

#4 Community Connections

Resource

Jim Liddle, Assistant Principal
Dublin Scioto High School
400 Hard Rd.
Dublin, OH 43016
E-Mail: Liddle_jim2mail.Dublin.k12.oh.us

Keep in Mind

- Pick your battles wisely. Becoming involved in every issue in the school is an exhausting, time-consuming, and impossible task.
- Listen carefully to the language of the person who is seeking your counsel.
- Ask yourself: "Is this an issue that I need to become involved in?"
- Ask the person if they want you to take action. Many times people just want to be heard and acknowledged.

Honor Students' Best Behavior

Goals

- Recognize good behavior as a quality that is just as important as academic achievement.
- Set a tone that good behavior is a significant contribution to the vision and culture of the school.
- Teach students that good citizenship is a way to honor their school, community, and nation.
- Make sure all students are eligible for this award, not just academic achievers.

Links with Other ISLLC Standards

#1 Vision Values
#2 Culture Counts
#3 Safe and Sound
#4 Community Connections
#6 Politics, Please

Resource

Walker Valley High School
750 Lauderdale Memorial Highway
Cleveland, TN 37312
Web site: www.walkervalleyhigh.com

Keep in Mind

- This strategy promotes the principal as a person who honors good behavior and defines the principal's role as more than just disciplinarian.
- The award exhibits fair behavior toward students and recognizes children who are often overlooked.
- Make sure staff members are involved in the selection of recipients.
- These awards are separate from end-of-the-grading-period award assemblies.

Change the School Climate
"One Child at a Time"

Goals

- Send a message to the entire community that behavior is a top priority within the culture of the school.
- Teach students that good citizenship is a way to honor their school, community, and nation.
- Make sure all students are eligible for this award, not just academic achievers.

Links with Other ISLLC Standards

#1 Vision Values

#2 Culture Counts

#3 Safe and Sound

#4 Community Connections

#6 Politics, Please

Resource

Debra Odom, Principal
Linmoor Middle School
2001 Hamilton Ave.
Columbus, OH 43211
E-mail: dodom@columbus.k12.oh.us

Keep in Mind

- Students who are "caught being good" are called to the office during morning PA announcements.
- Students whose behavior is marginal are encouraged to do the right thing.
- Students who challenge authority are given an opportunity to make a change, even if it is little by little.

Create a Diverse Environment

Goals

- Be sure that tolerance of diversity is highly visible in the school.
- Enlist all community members as participants in changing the school.
- Set a tone that diversity is highly honored within the framework of the school's vision and culture.

Links with Other ISLLC Standards

#1 Vision Values

#2 Culture Counts

#3 Safe and Sound

#4 Community Connections

#6 Politics, Please

Resource

Shapiro, S., Skinulis, K., & Skinulis, R. (2000). *Classrooms that work: A teacher's guide to discipline without stress.* Toronto: Practical Parenting, Inc. (Toll Free Number: (877) 210-0593.)

Keep in Mind

- Exhibit pictures, paintings, and posters of teachers from various backgrounds in classroom settings with children from ethnic groups different from that of the teacher.
- Diversity workshops can be held for staff and students during each semester to make sure that this very contemporary issue is in the forefront of the school's vision and culture.
- Display hall, entrance, exit, and restroom signs in multiple languages.

Take a Hard Look at the School Handbook

Goals

- Make sure the handbook is in alignment with the vision and culture of the school.
- Establish the handbook as a guideline for the day-to-day issues that arise.
- Refer to the handbook as a blueprint for any legal issues surrounding student conduct.

Links with Other ISLLC Standards

#1 Vision Values

#2 Culture Counts

#3 Safe and Sound

#4 Community Connections

#6 Politics, Please

Resource

Steven E. Raines, Executive Director
The Ohio Association of Secondary School Administrators
8050 N High Street, Suite 180
Columbus, OH 43235-6484
Web site: www.oassa.org

Keep in Mind

- Make sure the language of the handbook is in an easy-to-read format, free of educational jargon.
- A Student Code of Conduct should be included. The Student Code should be approved by the local elected school board every year.
- Student infractions that carry consequences of suspension or expulsion need to include the term "may" not "will," unless your school has a zero tolerance provision.

6

Politics, Please: ISLLC Standard 6

"A school administrator is an educational leader who pro-motes the success of all students by understanding, respond-ing to, and influencing the larger political, social, economic, legal, and cultural context."

Ensure Cultural Inclusiveness

Goals

- Serve as a resource for parents and students to learn English as a second language.
- Welcome parents into the American culture in a nonthreatening manner.
- Provide the larger community with a valuable educational resource.

Links with Other ISLLC Standards

#1 Vision Value
#2 Culture Count
#3 Safe and Sound

#4 Community Connections
#5 Ethics Embodied

Resources

U.S. Department of Education
400 Maryland Avenue, SW, Washington, D.C. 20202
Phone: (800) USA-LEARN
Web site: www.ed.gov/pubs/SchProj

Balderas Elementary School
4625 East Florence, Fresno, CA 93725
Phone: (209) 456-6800

Keep in Mind

- Ninety-eight percent of the students at Balderas Elementary School in Fresno, California, belong to ethnic minorities. Evening English classes are offered for both parents and students to open communication between the school and the community.
- Translators are provided for each of the native languages.
- The school also offers parent workshops that are conducted in the languages spoken by the individual families.
- Since the program's implementation, there have been substantial increases in test scores and attendance.

Establish Parent Liaisons

Goals

- Assure the community that the school is committed to the public education and the welfare of all its students.
- Bring school resources directly to parents.

Links with Other ISLLC Standards

#1 Vision Values

#2 Culture Counts

#3 Safe and Sound

#4 Community Connections

#5 Ethics Embodied

Resources

Halford, J. M. (1996, April). How parent liaisons connect families to school. (Published by: Association for Supervision and Curriculum Development.) *Educational Leadership*, 53(7).

Timber Lane Elementary School

2737 West St., Falls Church, VA 22046

Phone: (703) 206-5300

Keep in Mind

- To increase family involvement, Timber Lane Elementary School hires liaisons that operate as a community-based branch of the staff.
- Liaisons work well in communities where multiple languages are spoken. Their responsibilities vary and may include helping parents get involved with English as a Second Language courses (ESL), job training networks, adult literacy programs, financial assistance groups, and medical services and therapists.

Implement the Kids Voting USA Program

Goals

- Provide students with hands-on involvement with the democratic process.
- Establish communication with a national organization dedicated to teaching students about elections.
- Provide students with a unique opportunity to witness their community's commitment to fair elections.

Links with Other ISLLC Standards

#1 Vision Values
#2 Culture Counts
#3 Safe and Sound
#4 Community Connections
#5 Ethics Embodied

Resource

Kids Voting USA
www.kidsvotingusa.org
Sponsored by: Johns S. & James L. Knight Foundation
State Farm Insurance
Home Depot
AOL Time Warner

Keep in Mind

- Kids Voting USA is a nonprofit, nonpartisan, grassroots organization working with schools and communities to enhance civic education.
- The organization provides youth a voting experience at official polls on election day.
- The Kids Voting USA curricula invites students into official polling sites on election day and gives students a real-life experience with the election process.

Host a "Make It, Take It" Night

Goals

- Educate parents about the importance of statewide curriculum standards.
- Provide information about the school reform movement and its impact on each child's education.
- Help parents provide learning activities at home in conjunction with academic standards.

Links with Other ISLLC Standards

#1 Vision Values
#2 Culture Counts
#3 Safe and Sound
#4 Community Connections
#5 Ethics Embodied

Resource

Collaborative Communication Group
1801 Connecticut Ave. NW
Third Floor
Washington, D.C. 20009
Phone: (202) 986-4959
Web site: www.publicengagment.com

Keep in Mind

- This event is a back-to-school night with a twist. It allows parents to visit with their child's teachers and learn about the new content standards, which will measure student academic progress.
- Parents take activities home that will help their children master these standards.
- As a result of this program, parents and staff start the school year "on the same page" regarding standards-based expectations.

Establish Cultural Support Groups

Goals

- Provide a network of friendships for students with like ethnic and cultural backgrounds.
- Give extra help in adapting to the American culture for students of different ethnic and cultural backgrounds.
- Acknowledge and celebrate the ethnicity of students participating in this program.

Links with Other ISLLC Standards

#1 Vision Values

#2 Culture Counts

#3 Safe and Sound

#4 Community Connections

#5 Ethics Embodied

Resource

Tom Woodford, Guidance Counselor
Hilliard Darby High School
4200 Leppert Rd.
Hilliard, OH 43026
E-mail: tom_woodford@fclass.hilliard.k23.oh.us

Keep in Mind

- Students who share a commonality in culture, race, or ethnicity come together to work with a counselor to share information, and also learn about cultural events pertinent to their particular culture.
- This group will also be trained to facilitate large group discussions surrounding diversity with students, staff, parents, and community members.

Hold Saturday Family Workshops in the High School

Goals

- Model good citizenship practices with families.
- Establish and maintain communication with a variety of community resources.
- Stress the importance of the school curriculum by promoting an alternative to suspension or expulsion.

Links with Other ISLLC Standards

#1 Vision Values   #4 Community Connections

#2 Culture Counts   #5 Ethics Embodied

#3 Safe and Sound

Resource

U. S. Department of Education
Office of Safe and Drug-Free Schools, News Branch
400 Maryland Avenue, SW, Washington, D.C. 20202
Phone: (202) 260-3943
Web site: www.governmentguide.com
Web site: www.cops.usdoj.gov

Keep in Mind

- This program is used as an alternative to suspension or expulsion when youth use tobacco, alcohol, or other drugs.
- It is also implemented for infractions such as curfew violation and truancy.
- The curriculum focuses on communication skills, parenting skills, decision making, and problem solving. It also informs family members about the harmful effects of drug use.
- Parents and students work on a Family Action Plan to implement once the workshop ends.
- The program is available at no charge to families whose school districts are members of the Safe and Drug-Free Schools Consortium.

Introduce School Uniforms

Goals

- Provide an even playing field for all students in relation to their socioeconomic status.
- Help focus on learning as the primary reason for attending school.
- Communicate that safety is a primary concern during the school day.

Links with Other ISLLC Standards

#1 Vision Values

#2 Culture Counts

#3 Safe and Sound

#4 Community Connections

#5 Ethics Embodied

Resource

Stan Embry, Principal
Columbus Africentric School, K-6
300 E. Livingston Ave.
Columbus, OH 43215
Phone: (614) 365-88675

Keep in Mind

- School uniforms can reduce distractions and disruptions among students.
- All students wear a dress shirt with dark green or black dress pants and black shoes.
- This policy prevents students from feeling alienated due to what they wear.
- The policy eliminates any gang paraphernalia from becoming a focus of the school day.

Establish a School E-mail List

Goals

- Expand communication options by keeping in touch with parents electronically.
- Make sure that in case of a local or national emergency, parents will be informed in a timely fashion about school events.
- Include stakeholders in the larger community as part of this e-mail list to increase the school's visibility in the public arena.

Links with Other ISLLC Standards

#1 Vision Values
#2 Culture Counts
#3 Safe and Sound
#4 Community Connections
#5 Ethics Embodied

Resource

Kyle Wolfe, Principal
Logan Elm High School
9575 Tarlton Rd.
Circleville, OH 43113
Phone: (740) 474-7503

Keep in Mind

- Parents and community members have the opportunity to sign up for a weekly e-mail communication from the school.
- Parents and community members will be sent school district news to their computer every Friday.
- Each week's e-mail will include news articles, dates for events, and any school information that is important for the community to know.

Keep Communication Strong with Local Businesses

Goals

- Engage the business community in the "business of school."
- Provide added financial resources for school programming.
- Provide networking opportunities with school personnel and local businesses.

Links with Other ISLLC Standards

#1 Vision Values   #4 Community Connections

#2 Culture Counts   #5 Ethics Embodied

#3 Safe and Sound

Resource

James Grube, Principal
Westland High School
146 Galloway Rd., Galloway, OH 343119
E-mail: James_Grube@swcs.k12.oh.us

Keep in Mind

- This business partnership allows the school to maintain relationships with community members who are active in the business community.
- During these monthly meetings, the principal communicates to the local business association pertinent information regarding updates to school programs and events within the school.
- The principal requests that the business association raise money for scholarships and school events.
- The principal gains an outside perspective on issues concerning the school.
- The school has an administrative representative on the business association's executive council.

Establish an SOS Program

Goals

- Focus on safety issues within the school and the larger community.
- Promote good citizenship by educating students about their responsibilities in the area of safety.
- Promote awareness to the community that the school takes safety seriously.

Links with Other ISLLC Standards

#1 Vision Values   #4 Community Connections

#2 Culture Counts   #5 Ethics Embodied

#3 Safe and Sound

Resource

Jane Vazquez, Principal
Pickerington Elementary School
775 Long Rd., Pickerington, OH 43147
E-mail: jane_vazquez@fc.pickerington.k12.oh.us

Keep in Mind

- The SOS Program (Safety A'Round the Schools) is designed to raise awareness of student safety. The Parent Teacher Organization creates a panel of parents involved in helping to make the school a "kid safe" building.
- Educational programs are provided throughout the course of the year. Many times these include the police and fire departments.
- Concerns are brought up to the building principal through an advisory council.
- The PTO also looks at playground safety issues as well as various safety issues that relate to students' lives at home.

Participate in a "Take It to the Bank" Program

Goals

- Encourage Latino and Spanish language students to explore banking as a profession.
- Encourage corporate mentoring with the schools.
- Give special recognition to the United States' second largest population.
- Educate students on the free enterprise system.

Links with Other ISLLC Standards

#1 Vision Values

#2 Culture Counts

#3 Safe and Sound

#4 Community Connections

#5 Ethics Embodied

Resources

James Grube, Principal
Westland High School
146 Galloway Rd.
Galloway, OH 43119
E-mail:
James_Grube@swcs.k12.oh.us

Bank One Academy
academy@bankone.com
Big Brothers/Sisters
Web site:
bbbscolumbus.org

Keep in Mind

The Bank One Academy program selects a combination of 30 Latino and fourth-year Spanish students to participate.

- Employee volunteers from Bank One Corporation serve as mentors.
- Program partner, Big Brothers/Big Sisters, matches mentors and students on a one-to-three ratio.
- Interactive mentoring sessions take place over the course of one academic calendar year and are held at Bank One facilities.
- Session curriculum covers life skills, career skills, and financial literacy (including college financial aid).
- Students who successfully complete the program receive college or technical school scholarships and an opportunity for employment.

Pay Close Attention
to Special Education Issues

Goals

- Provide quality education for all students.
- Encourage tolerance for children with special needs.
- Promote outside agency participation in the educational process.

Links with Other ISLLC Standards

#1 Vision Values

#2 Culture Counts

#3 Safe and Sound

#4 Community Connections

#5 Ethics Embodied

Resource

Peggy McMurry, Principal
Big Walnut Elementary School
940 S. 3C Highway
Sunbury, OH 43074
E-mail: peggy_mcmurry@bigwalnut.k12.oh.us

Keep in Mind

- Public policy must be shaped to provide quality education for all students. One way to accomplish this task is to develop a special education unit.
- To develop a unit, research funding options and work to ensure that the school building is fit for an MH unit.
- Provide the necessary resources for the teacher, including classroom aides, training, and possibly a registered nurse.

Monitor Special Education Laws in Your State

Goals

- Ensure that all legal policies surrounding the school's special education program are being followed.
- Serve as a consultant when staff and parents have questions or concerns about special education provisions.

Links with Other ISLLC Standards

#1 Vision Values

#2 Culture Counts

#3 Safe and Sound

#4 Community Connections

#5 Ethics Embodied

Resource

Steve Mazzi, Principal
Big Walnut Middle School
105 Baughman St., PO Box 5002
Sunbury, OH 43074
E-mail: steve_mazzi@bigwalnut.k12.oh.us

Keep in Mind

- Follow all current litigation for special education through state/national principal associations.
- Establish a paper trail to ensure that all goals of each child's IEP are being met.
- Attend all Intervention Assistance Team (IAT) meetings.
- Incorporate other meetings throughout the school year to check on student progress. Encourage modification of IEPs when needed.
- Use the paper trail so that all goals are carried out to the fullest extent possible.

Be Aware of Your Belief System about Middle Schools

Goals

- Encourage self-reflection about legal, moral, and educational aspects of middle school learning.
- Focus on diversity within the student population.
- Set the tone for everyone in the school community to examine their beliefs about middle schools.

Links with Other ISLLC Standards

#1 Vision Values

#2 Culture Counts

#3 Safe and Sound

#4 Community Connections

#5 Ethics Embodied

Resource

Carol King, Principal
John Sells Middle School
150 W. Bridge St., Dublin, OH 43017
E-mail: king_carol@msmail.dublin.kk12.oh.us

Keep in Mind

- The personal belief system of the principal should revolve around a student-centered concept.
- An administrator should be available to help students, not just run a building.
- Students need to feel like they are part of something special and know that school is a community, not just a place to learn.
- Students need to be asked: "What kind of school do you want?"
- Meet with groups of students to see what they think and feel about their building. Give them ownership by making them part of the decision-making team.

Bring Compassion to School

Goals

- Prepare students for citizenship in a global community.
- Establish a sense of family within the school community.
- Emphasize trust and respect in the daily life of the school.
- Respect differences in all students, teachers, and parents.
- Keep school a safe haven for students with family difficulties.

Links with Other ISLLC Standards

#1 Vision Values   #4 Community Connections

#2 Culture Counts   #5 Ethics Embodied

#3 Safe and Sound

Resource

Julie Kenney, Principal, St. Vincent de Paul School
206 E. Chestnut St., Mt. Vernon, OH 43050
E-mail: jkenney@cdeducation.org

Keep in Mind

- "Dress Down Day" is held once a month, and students pay for the privilege to dress down. All monies are donated to supporting underprivileged children in a school-sponsored country.
- Students visit local environmental centers to learn about how the greater environmental world has an impact on daily lives.
- A buddy system is established in which new students and families are matched up with existing members of the school.
- A Safety Town program is initiated that pairs older and younger students together in a curriculum designed around traffic safety.

Sip Java with Jeff and Julie

Goals

- The school district focus is presented to parents and students.
- Poetry is shared as a way of publicizing the district goals.
- Networking with other parents, students, and administrators assists in creating community solidarity.
- Administrators provide an informal atmosphere for adult and student learning.

Links with Other ISLLC Standards

#1 Vision Values
#2 Culture Counts
#4 Community Connections
#5 Ethics Embodied

Resource

Jeff Brown, Principal
Oak Creek Elementary School
1256 Westwood Dr.
Lewis Center, OH 43035
E-mail: j_brown@olentangy.k12.oh.us

Keep in Mind

- Students and their families are invited to attend a poetry reading in the evening held by Principal Jeff Brown and Assistant Principal Julie Lather.
- Poems are read by both Jeff and Julie.
- Poems are chosen based on the focus of the district.
- Adults enjoy a cup of java and students sip hot cocoa during the poetry reading.

Bring the Wide World to School

Goals

- Emphasize and encourage equity and diversity in the school.
- Welcome diverse groups.
- Establish and maintain lines of communication with all groups within the larger community.

Links with Other ISLLC Standards

#1 Vision Values	#4 Community Connections
#2 Culture Counts	#5 Ethics Embodied
#3 Safe and Sound	

Resource

Gail Buick, Principal
Salem Elementary School
1040 Garvey Rd., Columbus, OH 43229
Phone: (614) 365-5351

Keep in Mind

- A schoolwide diversity festival is held that focuses on different countries, cultures, and celebrations.
- Each classroom represents a country and hosts a booth showcasing its selected country. The countries chosen represent the student population.
- Parents and community members help by explaining customs, clothing, artifacts, and music.
- Assign two ambassadors from each classroom to host a booth for the day, carry their country's flag in an assembly, and greet their guests in the language of their country.
- All students tour the various countries by presenting premade passports to be stamped upon "arrival." The completed passports allow students to sample authentic foods in the school cafeteria.

Organize a Student Leader Team

Goals

- Help students serve as role models for their peers.
- Get children interested in the satisfaction of volunteer work.
- Give all students a chance to show their leadership abilities.
- Reinforce the school vision and mission with productive volunteer work.
- Keep the daily school management running smoothly with volunteer help from students.

Links with Other ISLLC Standards

#1 Vision Values	#4 Community Connections
#2 Culture Counts	#5 Ethics Embodied
#3 Safe and Sound	

Resource

Kristin Whiting, Principal
Maybury Elementary School
2633 Maybury Rd., Columbus, OH 43232
E-mail: kwhiting@columbus.k12.oh.us

Keep in Mind

- Form a student leader team made up of representatives from each grade level.
- Instead of targeting only the "good" kids for the program, all students may apply by completing an application, which includes adult references.
- Fifty students are chosen. These students have to maintain grades, comply with dress codes, follow the rules, lead by good example, and have no disciplinary referrals.
- Jobs such as PA announcers, school beautification consultants, playground equipment managers, and recess and lunchroom helpers are designated.

View a Child's Perspective

Goals

- Give students a sense of ownership and pride in their school.
- Provide an artistic, welcoming atmosphere for all who enter the school.
- Focus on the arts as a form of self-expression.
- Invite community members to participate in a worthy school activity.

Links with Other ISLLC Standards

#1 Vision Values

#2 Culture Counts

#3 Safe and Sound

#4 Community Connections

Resource

Jeff Brown, Principal
Oak Creek Elementary School
1256 Westwood Dr., Lewis Center, OH 43035
E-mail: j_brown@olentangy.k12.oh.us

Keep in Mind

- Students participate by grade level in a mural contest that represents the school's social, economic, and cultural diversity.
- Winners will have their mural placed in the lobby's display case for the months of September and October.
- At the end of October, the mural will be auctioned off to staff, parents, or interested community members.
- The proceeds will go to purchasing food items that will be donated to the local food bank.

Design Multiple Community Efforts on Behalf of the School

Goals

- Involve all students in a productive after-school activity.
- Engage the community in a career-based project.
- Help students develop appropriate community role models.
- Focus on learning in a relaxed, after-school atmosphere.

Links with Other ISLLC Standards

#1 Vision Values
#2 Culture Counts
#3 Safe and Sound
#4 Community Connections
#5 Ethics Embodied

Resource

Andrew J. Smith III, Principal
Cassady Alternative Elementary School
2500 N Cassady Ave., Columbus, OH 43219
E-mail: ansmith@columbus.k12.oh.us

Keep in Mind

- Local churches provide mentoring to individual students as well as after-school activities.
- Local businesses allow older students to experience the workplace environment and explore career possibilities.
- Area firefighters provide life skills activities and special events for students and the entire community.
- A local college provides GED classes and personal finance workshops to adults in the neighborhood.

7

Appendix

You Can't Have One Without the Other

The ISLLC standards provide a much-needed roadmap for educational leaders. The broad themes of each standard permit latitude and diversity in how each standard may be implemented.

However, by the very nature of the breadth and depth of each standard, confusion has arisen about the concrete definition of each one. Does one theme emerge for each standard? The answer is yes. However, the complexity of educating children is so profound that these strategies have many layers. As strategies for this book were written, it became very clear that "no ISLLC standard is an island unto itself." Each standard carries with it underlying themes that tie into other standards.

School Culture: The Invisible Giant

The ISLLC standard that appears again and again throughout the entire course of this book is Standard #2: Culture Counts. It is ironic that in this data-driven world of contemporary American education, the intangible idea of school culture, or as Roland Barth states, "the way we do things around here," stands out in every facet of school life.

Each school has unique ways of going about its daily life. Issues that are hidden beneath the surface—including rituals, unspoken mores, and political land mines—are not readily visible to a new principal or even veteran administrators. As a result, determining the school culture accurately can make or break any educational leader's efforts at school reform.

Toxic school culture does not go away. It does not change overnight. Theoretically it can be changed in a year, but if the change is not deep and lasting, it will quickly revert back to the old way. And certainly the wise educational leader, in order to survive and thrive both professionally and personally, must acknowledge this invisible giant if real change is to take place.

There's an Army Out There to Help

The ISLLC standards and all the issues they encompass can be overwhelming. Any principal who reads this book may ask: "How can I accomplish this? It's impossible!" That is true. No one can do all of this alone. Just as no ISLLC standard is an island, neither is the principal.

Our mothers may have taught us, "If you want to do something right, do it yourself." However, for school principals this adage does not apply (maybe mother did not always know best). To educate children, it takes an army—an army of teacher leaders who look to the principal to set a tone of student achievement, not dictate or micromanage the school.

Teacher leaders possess inspirational ideas, political savvy, the ability to communicate well with students, and extraordinary vision of how to run a successful school. The wise principal listens to them, nurtures them, and recites this mantra: "All of us are smarter than one of us." Belief in this mantra can change the student achievement level in a school from average to spectacular.

In addition, teachers are keenly perceptive about the sincerity of their leaders. The principal must check his or her ego at the door and embrace the notion that the title of "principal" is the easy part. The title of "leader" occurs only when others are given the latitude to be leaders as well.

For all educational leaders who describe themselves as "control freaks," it is a mighty task to give up the lead and once in a while become a follower. It is a lesson that must be learned again and again throughout the course of the principal's career.

What Next for ISLLC?

As the ISLLC Standards become more and more embedded in the culture of American educational administration, it will become necessary to provide up-to-date strategies that all principals can use on the job. This book is only a beginning. It is hoped that it will serve to assist school administrators in their mission of educating our children, our nation's future.

For Further Reading

Hackmann, D. G., Schmitt-Oliver, D. M., and Tracy, J. C. (2002). *The standards-based administrative internship: Putting the ISLLC standards into practice.* Lanham, MD: Scarecrow Press.

Hessel, K., and Holloway, J. (2002). *A framework for school leaders: Linking the ISLLC standards to practice.* Princeton, NJ: Educational Testing Service.

Interstate School Leaders Licensure Consortium (1996). *Standards for school leaders.* Washington, DC: Council of Chief State School Officers.

National Commission on Excellence in Education (1983). *A nation at risk: The imperative for educational reform.* Washington, DC: U.S. Department of Education.

National Policy Board for Educational Administration (1989). *Improving the preparation of school administrators: An agenda for reform.* Charlottesville, VA: University of Virginia Press.

The Complete ISLLC Standards for School Leaders

Standard 1

A school administrator is an educational leader who promotes the success of all students by facilitating the development, articulation, implementation, and stewardship of a vision of learning that is shared and supported by the school community.

Knowledge

The administrator has knowledge and understanding of:

- Learning goals in a pluralistic society.
- The principles of developing and implementing strategic plans.
- Systems theory.
- Information sources, data collection, and data analysis strategies.
- Effective communication.
- Effective consensus-building and negotiation skills.

Dispositions

The administrator believes in, values, and is committed to:

- The educability of all.
- A school vision of high standards of learning.
- Continuous school improvement.
- The inclusion of all members of the school community.
- Ensuring that students have the knowledge, skills, and values needed to become successful adults.
- A willingness to continuously examine one's own assumptions, beliefs, and practices.
- Doing the work required for high levels of personal and organizational performance.

Performances

The administrator facilitates processes and engages in activities ensuring that:

- The vision and mission of the school are effectively communicated to staff, parents, students, and community members.
- The vision and mission are communicated through the use of symbols, ceremonies, stories, and similar activities.
- The core beliefs of the school vision are modeled for all stakeholders.
- The vision is developed with and among stakeholders.

- Contributions of school community members toward the realization of the vision are recognized and celebrated.
- Progress toward the vision and mission is communicated to all stakeholders.
- The school community is involved in school improvement efforts.
- The vision shapes the educational programs, plans, and actions.
- An implementation plan is developed in which objectives and strategies to achieve the vision and goals are clearly articulated.
- Assessment data related to student learning are used to develop the school vision and goals.
- Relevant demographic data pertaining to students and their families are used in developing the school mission and goals.
- Barriers to achieving the vision are identified, clarified, and addressed.
- Needed resources are sought and obtained to support the implementation of the school mission and goals.
- Existing resources are used in support of the school vision and goals.
- The vision, mission, and implementation plans are regularly monitored, evaluated, and revised.

Standard 2

A school administrator is an educational leader who promotes the success of all students by advocating, nurturing, and sustaining a school culture and instructional program conducive to student learning and professional growth.

Knowledge

The administrator has knowledge and understanding of:
- Student growth and development.
- Applied learning theories.
- Applied motivational theories.

- Curriculum design, implementation, evaluation, and refinement.
- Principles of effective instruction.
- Measurement, evaluation, and assessment strategies.
- Diversity and its meaning for educational programs.
- Adult learning and professional development models.
- The change process for systems, organizations, and individuals.
- The role of technology in promoting student learning and professional growth.
- School cultures.

Dispositions

The administrator believes in, values, and is committed to: Student learning as the fundamental purpose of schooling.
- The proposition that all students can learn.
- The variety of ways in which students can learn.
- Lifelong learning for self and others.
- Professional development as an integral part of school improvement.
- The benefits that diversity brings to the school community.
- A safe and supportive learning environment.
- Preparing students to be contributing members of society.

Performances

The administrator facilitates processes and engages in activities ensuring that:
- All individuals are treated with fairness, dignity, and respect.
- Professional development promotes a focus on student learning consistent with the school vision and goals.
- Students and staff feel valued and important.
- The responsibilities and contributions of each individual are acknowledged.
- Barriers to student learning are identified, clarified, and addressed.

- Diversity is considered in developing learning experiences.
- Lifelong learning is encouraged and modeled.
- There is a culture of high expectations for self, student, and staff performance.
- Technologies are used in teaching and learning.
- Student and staff accomplishments are recognized and celebrated.
- Multiple opportunities to learn are available to all students.
- The school is organized and aligned for success.
- Curricular, co-curricular, and extracurricular programs are designed, implemented, evaluated, and refined.
- Curriculum decisions are based on research, expertise of teachers, and the recommendations of learned societies.
- The school culture and climate are regularly assessed.
- A variety of sources of information is used to make decisions.
- Student learning is assessed using a variety of techniques.
- Multiple sources of information regarding performance are used by staff and students.
- A variety of supervisory and evaluation models is employed.
- Pupil personnel programs are developed to meet the needs of students and their families.

Standard 3

A school administrator is an educational leader who promotes the success of all students by ensuring management of the organization, operations, and resources for a safe, efficient, and effective learning environment.

Knowledge

The administrator has knowledge and understanding of:

- Theories and models of organizations and the principles of organizational development.
- Operational procedures at the school and district level.
- Principles and issues relating to school safety and security.
- Human resources management and development.
- Principles and issues relating to fiscal operations of school management.
- Principles and issues relating to school facilities and use of space.
- Legal issues impacting school operations.
- Current technologies that support management functions.

Dispositions

The administrator believes in, values, and is committed to:
- Making management decisions to enhance learning and teaching.
- Taking risks to improve schools.
- Trusting people and their judgments.
- Accepting responsibility.
- High-quality standards, expectations, and performances.
- Involving stakeholders in management processes.
- A safe environment.

Performances

The administrator facilitates processes and engages in activities ensuring that:
- Knowledge of learning, teaching, and student development is used to inform management decisions.
- Operational procedures are designed and managed to maximize opportunities for successful learning.
- Emerging trends are recognized, studied, and applied as appropriate.
- Operational plans and procedures to achieve the vision and goals of the school are in place.

- Collective bargaining and other contractual agreements related to the school are effectively managed.
- The school plant, equipment, and support systems operate safely, efficiently, and effectively.
- Time is managed to maximize attainment of organizational goals.
- Potential problems and opportunities are identified.
- Problems are confronted and resolved in a timely manner.
- Financial, human, and material resources are aligned to the goals of schools.
- The school acts entrepreneurially to support continuous improvement.
- Organizational systems are regularly monitored and modified as needed.
- Stakeholders are involved in decisions affecting schools.
- Responsibility is shared to maximize ownership and accountability.
- Effective problem-framing and problem-solving skills are used.
- Effective conflict resolution skills are used.
- Effective group-process and consensus-building skills are used.
- Effective communication skills are used.
- A safe, clean, and aesthetically pleasing school environment is created and maintained.
- Human resource functions support the attainment of school goals.
- Confidentiality and privacy of school records are maintained.

Standard 4

A school administrator is an educational leader who promotes the success of all students by collaborating with families and community members, responding to diverse community interests and needs, and mobilizing community resources.

Knowledge

The administrator has knowledge and understanding of:

- Emerging issues and trends that potentially impact the school community.
- The conditions and dynamics of the diverse school community.
- Community resources.
- Community relations and marketing strategies and processes.
- Successful models of school, family, business, community, government, and higher education partnerships.

Dispositions

The administrator believes in, values, and is committed to:

- Schools operating as an integral part of the larger community.
- Collaboration and communication with families.
- Involvement of families and other stakeholders in school decision-making processes.
- The proposition that diversity enriches the school.
- Families as partners in the education of their children.
- The proposition that families have the best interests of their child in mind.
- Resources of the family and community needing to be brought to bear on the education of students.
- An informed public

Performances

The administrator facilitates processes and engages in activities ensuring that:

- High visibility, active involvement, and communication with the larger community is a priority.
- Relationships with community leaders are identified and nurtured.

- Information about family and community concerns, expectations, and needs is used regularly.
- There is outreach to different business, religious, political, and service agencies and organizations.
- Credence is given to individuals and groups whose values and opinions may conflict.
- The school and community serve one another as resources.
- Available community resources are secured to help the school solve problems and achieve goals.
- Partnerships are established with area businesses, institutions of higher education, and community groups to strengthen programs and support school goals.
- Community youth family services are integrated with school programs.
- Community stakeholders are treated equitably.
- Diversity is recognized and valued.
- Effective media relations are developed and maintained.
- A comprehensive program of community relations is established.
- Public resources and funds are used appropriately and wisely.
- Community collaboration is modeled for staff.
- Opportunities for staff to develop collaborative skills are provided.

Standard 5

A school administrator is an educational leader who promotes the success of all students by acting with integrity, fairness, and in an ethical manner.

Knowledge

The administrator has knowledge and understanding of:
- The purpose of education and the role of leadership in modern society.
- Various ethical frameworks and perspectives on ethics.

- The values of the diverse school community.
- Professional codes of ethics.
- The philosophy and history of education.

Dispositions

The administrator believes in, values, and is committed to:
- The ideal of the common good.
- The principles in the Bill of Rights.
- The right of every student to a free, quality education.
- Bringing ethical principles to the decision-making process.
- Subordinating one's own interest to the good of the school community.
- Accepting the consequences for upholding one's principles and actions.
- Using the influence of one's office constructively and productively in the service of all students and their families.
- Developing a caring school community.

Performances

The administrator:
- Examines personal and professional values.
- Demonstrates a personal and professional code of ethics.
- Demonstrates values, beliefs, and attitudes that inspire others to higher levels of performance.
- Serves as a role model.
- Accepts responsibility for school operations.
- Considers the impact of one's administrative practices on others.
- Uses the influence of the office to enhance the educational program rather than for personal gain.
- Treats people fairly, equitably, and with dignity and respect.
- Protects the rights and confidentiality of students and staff.

- Demonstrates appreciation for and sensitivity to the diversity in the school community
- Recognizes and respects the legitimate authority of others.
- Examines and considers the prevailing values of the diverse school community.
- Expects that others in the school community will demonstrate integrity and exercise ethical behavior.
- Opens the school to public scrutiny.
- Fulfills legal and contractual obligations.
- Applies laws and procedures fairly, wisely, and considerately.

Standard 6

A school administrator is an educational leader who promotes the success of all students by understanding, responding to, and influencing the larger political, social, economic, legal, and cultural context.

Knowledge

The administrator has knowledge and understanding of:
- Principles of representative governance that undergird the system of American schools.
- The role of public education in developing and renewing a democratic society and an economically productive nation.
- The law as related to education and schooling.
- The political, social, cultural, and economic systems and processes that impact schools.
- Models and strategies of change and conflict resolution as applied to the larger political, social, cultural, and economic contexts of schooling.
- Global issues and forces affecting teaching and learning.
- The dynamics of policy development and advocacy under our democratic political system.

- The importance of diversity and equity in a democratic society.

Dispositions

The administrator believes in, values, and is committed to:
- Education as a key to opportunity and social mobility.
- Recognizing a variety of ideas, values, and cultures.
- Importance of a continuing dialog with other decision makers affecting education.
- Actively participating in the political and policy-making context in the service of education.
- Using legal systems to protect student rights and improve student opportunities.

Performances

The administrator facilitates processes and engages in activities ensuring that:
- The environment in which schools operate is influenced on behalf of students and their families.
- Communication occurs among the school community concerning trends, issues, and potential changes in the environment in which schools operate.
- There is ongoing dialog with representatives of diverse community groups.
- The school community works within the framework of policies, laws, and regulations enacted by local, state, and federal authorities.
- Public policy is shaped to provide quality education for students.
- Lines of communication are developed with decision makers outside the school community.

Source: Interstate School Leaders Licensure Consortium. (1996). *Standards for school leaders*. Washington, DC: Council of Chief State School Officers.